Matthew Hale

A short Treatise touching Sheriffs Accompts

Matthew Hale

A short Treatise touching Sheriffs Accompts

ISBN/EAN: 9783743345072

Manufactured in Europe, USA, Canada, Australia, Japa

Cover: Foto ©ninafisch / pixelio.de

Manufactured and distributed by brebook publishing software (www.brebook.com)

Matthew Hale

A short Treatise touching Sheriffs Accompts

A SHORT TREATISE

Rob: Touching *Cromer*

Sheriffs Accompts.

Written by the Honourable Sir *Matthew Hale*, Kt. sometime Lord Chief Justice of His Majesty's Court of *King's-Bench*.

To which is added, A Tryal of Witches, at the Assizes held at *Bury St. Edmonds*, for the County of *Suffolk*, on the 10th of *March* 1664, before the said Sir *Matthew Hale*, Kt.

LONDON,

Printed, and are to be sold by *Will. Shrowsbery*, at the *Bible* in Duke-Lane. 1683.

FOR

The Right Honourable

THE

Lord High Treasurer

OF

ENGLAND,

And the

CHANCELLOR

Of the

EXCHEQUER.

Ccording to my Promise to your Lordships, I have given a large Historical Narrative of the Sheriffs Accompts for the

Annu-

Epistle Dedicatory.

Annual Revenue of their Countries: Wherein some things may occurr that may be usefull to the understanding of the Sheriffs Accompts, and many other old obscure Records, and some things incidently opened that have been formerly obscure and scarce intelligible, yet fit to be known. Some things also relating to the difference between the Auditors of the Revenue, and the Officers of the Pipe. There may be some mistakes of my own, I confess, in a matter of so great intricacy, perplexity and obsoleteness, which I could not easily correct, in the Country, because many

of

Epistle Dedicatory.

of my Papers are at *London* that concern this business, and, I fear, hardly to be retrieved into a due order, in regard of the late distraction. And here may be some mistakes in the Transcriber, which at this distance I could not examine. But, possibly, notwithstanding these mistakes, Your Lordships may find something that may be usefull, and when I wait upon you I shall review and correct.

Your Lordships

humble Servant.

THE

THE
CONTENTS.

CHAP. I.
Touching the Ancient and Modern Weight and Allay of Sterling Silver. Page 1.

CHAP. II.
Concerning the Weight of Coin, and the difference therein, with regard to the Denomination of Coin.

p. 14.

CHAP. III.
Touching the Corruptions of Money and the Remedies anciently used in relation thereunto. p. 19.

CHAP. IV.
Concerning the manner of answering the King's Firmes anciently.

p. 30.

CHAP. V.
Concerning the manner of collecting the King's Revenues of the County, and the several kinds of them, with their several Titles. p. 33.

CHAP.

The Contents.
CHAP. VI.
Concerning the manner how the Annual Revenue of the County was usually answered in the ancient times untill 10 E. 1.   p. 48.

CHAP. VII.
The Second Period of the Sheriffs Accompts, viz. *how they stood from* 10 E. 1. *untill* 34 H. 8.   p. 63.

CHAP. VIII.
Touching the state of the Sheriffs Firmes from the Statute of 34 H. 8. *till the* 14*th year of the Reign of King* Charles 1. *which is the Second Period.*   p. 77.

CHAP. IX.
The Third Period from the 15*th year of King* Charles 1. *untill the year of our Lord* 1650, *and how the Sheriffs Firmes and Accompts stood in that intervall.*   p. 87.

CHAP. X.
The Fourth Period of the Sheriffs Firmes from the year 1650 *unto this day and how they were answered in that intervall.*   p. 89.

A Short

A Short
TREATISE
Touching
Sheriffs Accompts.

CHAP. I.

Touching the ancient and modern Weight and Allay of Sterling Silver.

IT will be neceſſary for the better underſtanding of Sheriffs accompts, eſpecially in the elder times, to examine theſe matters, *viz.*

I. Touching the Denomination, Weight and Allay of Sterling Money,

ney, the Corruptions thereof in both, and the remedies that have been formerly applied for the reformation of these corruptions.

II. Concerning Firmes, their nature, and how they were answered in former times. The first shall be the subject of this Chapter, the second the subject of the next.

Concerning the former of these, I shall apply my self singly to the business of Silver Coin, because that was the usual species wherein the King's Firmes were commonly answered.

And first, concerning the Coin of Silver, there are these things considerable therein.

1. The Authority or Power that gives it its Stamp, Weight, Denomination and Value.
2. The Matter of it.
3. The Weight and Denomination.

As concerning the first of these, it is, without all question, the inherent Regality and Prerogative of the Crown, to give the Currantness,

ness, Allay, Weight, Denomination and extrinfique Value to the Coin of this Kingdom: and as it is a part of his Regality and Prerogative, so it is a part of his Regal Revenue, which is called the King's Seigniorage, or Royalty, or Coinage, *viz.* ordinarily, on every pound weight of Gold, the King had for his Coin 5*s.* out of which he paid to the Master of the Mint, for his work, sometimes 1*s.* sometimes 1*s.* 6*d.* Upon every pound weight of Silver, the Seigniorage, or Coinage, answered to the King, in the time of King *Edw.* 3. was 8 peny weight, *pondere*, which about that time amounted to 1*s.* out of which he paid sometimes 8*d.* sometimes 9*d.* to the Master. In the time of *H.* 5. the King's Seigniorage of every pound weight of Silver was 15*d.* See *Rot. Parl.* 9 *H.* 5. *pars* 2. *N.* 15. although the Authorization, Denomination and Stamp of Coin was undoubtedly the King's right, yet it appears by *Roger Hawood*, that in the troublesome times of King *Stephen*

Stephen, *viz. An. Dom.* 1149. *Omnes Potentes, tam Episcopi quam Comites & Barones, suam faciebant monetam.* But *Henry* the second coming to the Crown, remedied this usurpation of the Baronage: *Novam fecit monetam quæ sola recepta erat & accepta in regno.* And since that time, the exercise as well as the right of coining of Money in the Kingdom hath remained uninterruptedly in the Crown. It is true, that by certain ancient privileges, derived by Charter and Usage from the Crown, divers, especially of the eminent Clergy, had their Mints or Coinages of Money. As the Abbot of St. *Edmunds-bury, Clauf.* 32 *H.* 8. *m.* 15. *dorso*: And the Archbishop of *York Clauf.* 5 *E.* 3. *pars* 1. *m.* 10. 19. *dorso*, and some others. But although they had the profit of the Coin, yet they had neither the Denomination Stamp, nor Allay: for upon every change of the Coin by the King's Proclamation, there issued over a Mandate to the Treasurer

surer and Barons to deliver a Stamp over to those private Mints to be used. But this liberty of Coinage in private Lords hath been long since difused, and in a great measure, if not altogether, reassumed by the Statute of 3 *H. 7. Cap.* 6.

2. Concerning the second, *viz.* the Matter or Species whereof the currant Coin of this Kingdom hath been made, it is Gold or Silver, but not altogether pure, but with an Allay of Copper, at least from the time of King *H.* 1. and *H.* 2. though possibly in ancienter times the Species whereof the Coin was made might be pure Gold or Silver; and this Allay was that which gave the Denomination of Sterling to that Coin, *viz.* Sterling Gold, or Sterling Silver: Wherein there will be inquirable,

1. Whence that Denomination came.

2. How ancient that Denomination was.

3. What was the Allay that gave Silver that Denomination.

For

For the former of these there are various conjectures, and nothing of certainty.

Spelman supposeth it to take that Denomination from the *Esterlings,* who, as he supposeth, came over and reformed our Coin to that Allay. Of this opinion was *Cambden, A Germanis, quos Angli* Esterlings, *ab Orientali situ, vocarunt, facta est appellatio; quos* Johannes *Rex, ad Argentum in suam puritatem redigendam, primus evocavit: & ejusmodi nummi* Esterlingi, *in antiquis scripturis semper reperiuntur.* Some suppose that it might be taken up from the *Starre Judæorum,* who being the great Brokers for Money, accepted and allowed Money of that Allay, for currant payment of their Stars or obligations. Others from the impression of a Sterling, or of an Asterisck upon the Coin. *Pur ceo que le form d'un Stare, dont le diminutive est Sterling, fuit impresst ou stamp sur ceo.*

Auters pur ceo que le primer de cest Standard fuit coyn en le Castle de de Sterlin in Scotland *pur le Roy* Edw. 1. And possibly as the proper name of the fourth part of a Peny was called a Farthing, and ordinarily a Ferling; so in truth the proper name of a Peny in those times was called a Sterling, without any other reason of it than the use of the times and arbitrary imposition, as other names usually grow. For the old Act of 51 *H*. 3. called *Compositio Mensurarum*, tells us that *Denarius Angliæ Sterlingus dicitur.* And because this was the root of the measure, especially of Silver Coin, as will be shewed, therefore all our Coin of the same Allay was also called Sterling, as five Shillings Sterling, five Pounds Sterling.

2. When this name of Sterling came first in is uncertain, onely we are certain it was a Denomination in use in the time of *H*. 3. or *Ed*. 1. and after-ages. But it was not in use at the time of the compiling of Doomsday, for if it were we should have found it there, where there is

so great occasion of mention of Firmes, Rents and Payments.

Standard del mony en French est appel Pied de mony per Bodin, Pes monetarum, quasi Princeps ibi pedem figit.

Matth. Paris mag. Hist. 220. *b. In le* 12 *an. de Roy* John *le primier standard del English mony fuit establish en Realm d'* Ireland, *et fuit equal al primes, & que l' English mony ne fuit au quart part melior in value que l' Irish, come ceo ad estre depuis le temps del* Edw. 4. *Et fuit change in* Ireland *come ceo fuit change in* Engleterre. *Le primer difference & inequality inter les Standards del English monies, & Irish monies est troue in* 5 Ed. 4. *car donq; fuit declare in Parliament icy que le Noble serra currant en cest Realm pur* 10s. *& issint fuit que l' Irish Shilling forsque* 9d. *Dengletre.*

Hovenden *in Rich.* 1. *fol.* 377. *b. Videns igitur* Galfridus Eboracensis *electus, quod nisi mediante pecunia amorem Regis sui nullatenus habere possit,*

poſſit, promiſit ei tria millia Librarum Sterlingorum pro amore ejus habendo. Que fuit devant le temps del Roy John; *pur que ſemble que le temps quant ceſt money fuit primerment coin eſt uncertain. Car aſcuns diont que fuit fait per* Osbright *un Roy de* Saxon *race* 160 *ans devant le* Norman *conqueſt.* Nummus *a* Numa *que fuit le primer Roy que feſoit moneies en* Rome. *Iſſint Sterlings, alias Eſterlings, queux primes feſoient le money de ceſt Standard en* Engleterre.

3. As touching the Allay that is by uſe and cuſtom fitted to that Money which we call the Sterling, or Sterling Allay; perchance we ſhall not find that conſtancy in the Allay as is generally thought.

The Sterling Allay of Gold, according to the Red Book of the Exchequer is this. The Pound weight of Gold conſiſts of twenty four Charats, every Charat weighing half an Ounce of Silver; and every Charat of Gold conſiſts of four Grains, and conſequently every
Grain

Grain of Gold weighing thirty of these Grains which we call Silver Grains, whereof hereafter.

In the time of *Edw.* 3. the Pound of Sterling Gold consisted of twenty three Charats, three Grains and a half of pure Gold, and half a Grain of Allay of Copper.

The Sterling Silver, as it seems to me, in former times had an Allay differing from what it is at this day. At this day a Pound weight of Silver (*viz.* 12 Ounces to the Pound, or *Troy* weight) consists of eleven Ounces two Peny-weight of fine Silver, and eighteen Peny-weight of Allay or Copper: every Pound containing twelve Ounces, and every Ounce divided into 20 parts called twenty Peny-weight: For at that time 20 Peny-weight weighed one Ounce, which though the Peny-weight be altered, yet the Denomination continues. And this Allay was in use in the forty sixth year of King *Edw.* 3. and for some time before, and hath continued ever since.

In the Treatife of Money in the Red Book of the Exchequer which feems to be written in the time of *Edw.* 3. for it mentions the Indentures of the Mint in 23 *Ed.* 3. it is faid the ufe was then that in every pound weight of Sterling Silver there was fixteen Peny-weight of Allay: the confequence whereof is that the Pound of Sterling Silver then contained eleven Ounces four Peny-weight of fine Silver, and fixteen Peny-weight of Copper.

And it fhould feem by what follows in the Chapter, that in the time of *H.* 2. the Allay of Copper in Sterling Silver was lefs than that: For upon every Pound weight of Silver Money they ufed to allow 12 Peny-weight *ad dealbandam firmam*; which feems to be the remedy for the reduction of the Money then currant into fine Silver, *fed de hoc poftea*.

But at this day, and for very many reafons, the Allay of Sterling Silver hath been 18 Peny-weight of Copper allowed to 11 Ounces

2 Pe-

2 Peny-weight of fine Silver; thereby making up the Pound weight Troy of Sterling. *Vid.* Indentures of the Mint, *Clauf.* 46 *Ed.* 3. *m.* 18. *Dorf. Clauf.* 1. *H.* 5. *m.* 35. *Dorf. Clauf.* 4. *Ed.* 4. *m.* 20. And this I take at this day to continue the Standard of Sterling Silver.

    29 E. 1. *Per special ordinance del Roy les Pollards & Crockards fueront decrie & adnul, quel ordinance fuit transmit in Realm d'* Ireland *& enrol en Exchequer icy, come est troue in Libro rubro Scaccarii, ibid. pars* 2. *fol.* 2. *b.*

    En temps E. 1. *Denarius Angliæ, qui nominatur Sterlingus, rotundus sine tonsura, ponderabit triginta & duo grana in medio spicæ.*

    Sterlingus & Denarius sont tout un. Le Shilling consistoit de 12 *Sterlings.* 25 E. 3. cap. 6. *Le substance de cest denier ou* Sterling *Peny al primes fuit vicesima pars unciæ. Et issint continue tanq.* 9 E. 3. *quant l' ounce del Silver fuit tallie in* 26 *pence que proportion fuit conti-*

Dy. 6. &
7 Ed. 6.

Raftal Money. 345.

continue tanq. 2 H. 6. *quant l' ounce del Silver fefoit* 32 *pence. Et ceſt iuſq; al* 5 E. 4. *quant feſoit* 40 *pence. Et ceſt iuſques* 36 H. 8. *quant il prepare ſon journy al* Bulloigne & *donq; fuit divide en* 45 *pence. Que continue iuſques al* 2 El. *quant l' ounce de pure Silver fuit tallie en* 60 *pence, & ceſt Standard remain a ceſt jour.*   Davies 24.

Et quælibet libra de ſterling avoit 18d. ob. *d' allay de* Copper, & *nient plus. Et ceſt allay de ſterling Mony les Ordinances ou Statutes de* 25 E. 3. *cap.* 13. & 2 H. 6. *cap.* 13. *font mention, & eſt contein en touts Indentures fait enter le Roy & les Maiſters del Mint.*

CHAP.

CHAP. II.

Concerning the Weight of Coin, and the difference therein, with regard to the Denomination of Coin.

THE Pound weight of Gold though it were the same with that of Silver, yet is made up of smaller parts of a different Denomination, every Pound weight consisting of 24 Charats, and every Charat consisting of 4 Grains.

The Pound weight of Silver is subdivided into parts of another Denomination; for every Pound consists of 20 Peny-weights, and every Peny-weight of 24 Grains. This appears by the Books and Records above mentioned. *Et touts susdits moneys dargent issint faites serront dallay de Standard de veil Esterling: Cest ascavoir que chescun leivre dargent de cestes moneys de poize tiendra*

dra vnze ounces & 2d. de poize dargent fine, & 18d. de poys dallay, chefcun peny weight containant 24 grains.

So that every Charat in the Pound weight of Gold equals half an Ounce of Silver; and every Grain of Gold, the fourth part of a Charat, equals 60 Grains of Silver weight.

In that old Ordinance, before mentioned called *Compofitio Menfurarum* 51 *H.* 3. it is faid, *Per ordinationes totius Regni* Angliæ *fit una menfura Domini Regis compofita, viz. quod Denarius* Angliæ, *qui nominatur Sterlingus, rotundus fine tonfura ponderabit triginta & duo Grana frumenti in medio fpicæ; & viginti Denarii faciunt Vnciam; & duodecim Vnciæ faciunt Libram,* &c.

But thefe thirty two Grains in the middle of the ear of Corn, are the natural Grains, which were the weight of the then Englifh Sterling Peny. But for the better accommodation of Accompts, thefe 32 natural Grains are reduced to 24 artificial Grains, which

which, from very ancient time unto this day are the common measure of the Peny-weight, as the 20 Peny-weight is the measure of an Ounce.

Having thus stated the artificial weights of Gold, and Silver, especially the latter, I shall proceed to the comparison that now and anciently stands between these artificial weights and the Coin of Silver.

It is very plain that in the latter end of *H.* 3. and the beginning of King *Ed.* 1. and for a long time before, twenty Pence of Sterling Money did weigh an Ounce, and twelve times twenty Pence or twenty Shillings did then weigh a Pound Troy weight: and accordingly as twenty Peny-weight was then an Ounce, and so called, so two hundred forty Pence, or twenty Shillings was a Pound weight, and so called, *viz. Libra Argenti.* And although at this day the Peny and the 20 Shillings of Silver is much altered in their true weight, yet the Denomination is still retained. The Ounce is commonly divided and

estieftimated by 20 Peny-weight, and 20 Shillings is called *Libra Argenti*.

In the time of King *Edw.* 1. (as appears) an Ounce of Sterling Silver made 20 Sterling Pence, and confequently a Pound of Sterling Silver made 240 Pence Sterling. But procefs of time hath made a great alteration between the Weight and extrinfique Denomination or Value of Money.

·In 46 *E.* 3. it appears by the Indenture of the Mint that a Pound of Sterling Silver made then 300 Sterling Pence. *Clauf.* 46. *E.* 3. *m.* 18.

And afterwards in 1 *H.* 5. the reduction of Coin was fuch that a Pound weight of Sterling Silver made 360 Pence Sterling. *Clauf.* 1 *H.* 5. *m.* 35. *dorfo.* Which made the Pound weight of Silver to contain 30 Shillings, and deducting 1 Shilling for Coinage, the Merchant had 29 Shillings for his Pound of Silver brought into the Mint.

In the 4th year of *Ed.* 4. the Pound of Sterling Silver yielded 33 Shillings

viz.

viz. about 396 Pence in the Pound: and consequently 33 Sterling Pence then made the Ounce of Silver. *Clauſ.* 4. *E.* 4. *m.* 20.

At this day the Ounce of Silver coined contains 5 Shillings, or 60 Pence: and consequently the Pound weight of coined Silver yields 60 Sterlings or 720 pence. So that at this day the extrinſecal Denomination or Value of Money in proportion to its Weight, is three times higher than it was in the time of *E.* 1. And thus much ſhall ſuffice touching the ſecond enquiry.

CHAP.

CHAP. III.

Touching the Corruptions of Money, and the remedies anciently used in relation thereunto.

BY what hath been before said it appeareth, the two special requisites of the currant Coin of this Kingdom are,

I. That it be of the true Standard in relation to its weight.

II. Of the true Standard with relation to its Allay: and proportionably to these two requisites are these defects, which have hapned in Moneys in modern and ancient times, *viz.*

I. The defect in the due weight of Money which hapned sometimes by counterfeiting the Sterling Money, though with a weight below the Standard. Sometimes by clipping, or otherwise impairing the weight of true Money.

2. The defect in the due Allay : *viz.* overcharging the fine Silver or Gold with an Allay of Copper more than the Standard, which hapned sometimes by the deceit or ignorance of the officers of the Mint, and sometimes by the counterfeiture of the Coin of *England*.

And by these practices the King's Exchequer (into or through which the most of the Money of the Kingdom successively came) was many times surcharged with such defective Money, and the King thereby deceived in his Firmes.

And therefore in ancient times there were successive experiments made by the officers of the King's revenue for the discovery and avoiding of these defective Monies and that his Rents might be answered in Money of a just weight and Allay; which, for the better understanding of ancient Records, remain here to be explicated, *viz. Solutio ad Scalam, Solutio ad Pensum*, and Combustion, or tryal by fire.

fire. The two former being such Remedies as related to defective Weight, and the latter being the Remedy that relates to defect in the Standard of Allay. And, touching this business, although we have very frequent mention of them, in the Pipe-rolls especially, yet the best, and contemporary exposition of them is *Gervasius Tilburiensis*, or the black Book of the Exchequer, written in the time of *H.* 2. who gives us the accompt thereof in his first Book, *Cap. A quibus, & ad quid inventa fuit. Argenti examinatio*, who thus expounds it.

1. *Solutio ad Scalam,* viz. *præter quamlibet Libram numeratam sex Denarios*, which it seems was agreed upon a *medium* to be the common estimate or Remedy for the defective Weight of Money, thereby to avoid the trouble of weighing the Money which was brought into the Exchequer. And this is the meaning of that frequent expression in the ancient Pipe-rolls *In Thesauro* 100*l. ad Scalam,* which
seems

seems to be one hundred Pounds, and one hundred Sixpences, or fifty Shillings.

2. *Solutio ad Pensum*: which was the payment of Money into the Exchequer by full weight, *viz.* that a Pound, or 20*s.* in Silver, *numero*, or by tale, should not be received for a Pound unless it did exactly weigh a Pound weight Troy, or twelve Ounces, and if it wanted any, that then the Payer should make good the weight by adding other Money although it amounted to more or less than 6*d.* in the Pound (which was the *Solutio ad Scalam*, as before is mentioned.) And thus frequently occurs in the Pipe-rolls, *In Thesauro* 100*l. and pensum*, or full weight.

3. Combustion or tryal by fire: which is by *Gervase* supposed to be set on foot by the Bishop of *Salisbury*, then Treasurer, (though in truth it were much more ancient, as appears by frequent passages in the Book of Doomsday:) and the Author gives the reason: *Licet enim numero & pondere videretur esse satisfactum,*

tisfactum,. non tamen materia. Consequens enim non erat ut si pro Libra una numerata 20 *Solidos, etiam Libra ponderis respondentis consequenter Libram solvisset : Argentum enim Cupro vel quovis Ære solvisset.* And thereupon ensued the constitution of examination of Money at the Exchequer by Combustion. Whether this examination was to reduce an equation of Money onely to Sterling, *viz.* a due proportion of Allay with Copper; or to reduce it to fine and pure Silver, and to make the estimate of the Pound or *Libra Argenti*, reserved of their Firmes to be in pure Silver, and without Allay, doth not so clearly appear. Some think the former; and therefore that the old expression of *Firma alba*, blank Firm, and *dealbare Firmam*, was nothing else but Coin melted down and reduced to the Allay of Sterling, and after blanched, or whited, as is done by the Moneyers with their Sterling Coin of Silver, which is to this day called blanching. *Vid.* Spelman *in tit.*

tit. Firmam dealbare. But yet it may seem, by what ensues, that it was to reduce it to fine Silver, and to the estimate of the Pound, or *Libra Argenti* accordingly; for it is evident by what follows, that the difference between a Pound, or *Libra Argenti numero*, and *Libra Argenti blanch*, was 12 Pence in every Pound: which possibly might be that the allowed Allay of Copper in the Sterling Silver was then twelve Pence weight of Copper in the Pound of fine Silver, whereas it is now 18 Peny-weight in the Pound. This tryal of Silver by Combustion, in those elder ages soon prevailed and obtained against the former reductions *ad Scalam, & ad Pensum*, as being the onely infallible tryal of the truth of the Metal, whereby the former reductions of *Pensum* and *Scalam* became in time antiquated.

And this begat the distinction in the old Rolls of the estimate of Money *Numero*, and the estimate *Blanc:* and in pursuance thereto the reservations

vations of Rents and Firmes by the King were sometimes *Numero*, and sometimes *Blanc*.

The reservations of Rents *numero* were no other but so much Money reserved *in Pecuniis numeratis*: as *reddendo quinque Libras numero* was fivescore Shillings, which amounted in common estimation to five Pounds Troy weight: And this was the ancient and usual reservation, and, *prima facie*, unless the contrary were expressed, upon all Grants of Lands (reserving so much Rent) it was intended *numero*; that is, so much in Money numbred, and the Firmor was not bound *dealbare Firmam*, or to make good so much in fine Silver, or, if you will, in such silver as was of the first Allay.

The reservation of so much Money, or so many Pounds *blanc* did enforce the Firmor to make good to the King so much in fine Silver, (or at least in the purest Sterling) and therefore such Firmor, when he paid in his Firme upon such a reservation

vation *blanc*, was bound *dealbare Firmam*, which was to submit his Money to the test of the fire; and to answer his Money, and make it good in fine Silver according to the reservation, or to pay in allowance thereof that rate which was the ordinary measure of reduction of it to fine Silver, which was 12 *d.* for every Pound as shall be shewed.

And hereupon grew the common difference which is every-where mentioned in the Pipe-rolls of Firmes *numero*, and Firmes *blanc* or *alb.* Firme.

This difference of these Firmes is expounded by the Black Book of the Exchequer, *Lib.* 2. *Cap. Quid sit quosdam fundos dari* blanc, *quosdam numero, viz.* that if a Firme or Tenement were let by the King generally, without expressing *blanc* or *numero*, it was to be answered onely *numero*, unless specially reserved *blanc*, (*viz. 5s. blanc.*) But if a Royalty or Franchise were onely granted, then the general reservation of so much Rent, was to be *blanc* Rent.

Rent. - *Porro, Firmam numero dari diximus cum tantum numerando, non examinando ipso satisfit. Cum ergo Rex Firmam alicui contulerit, simul cum Hundredo vel placito quæ ex hoc proveniunt, Firma dealbari dicitur: sin simpliciter fundum dederit (non determinans cum Hundredo vel* blanc.) *numero datus dicitur.* And from this diversity of the Rents arising in any County (some *blanc* onely, some *numero* onely, some in both) arose the diversity in the titling of the Sheriffs Accompts, *viz.*

Firma de remanente Comitatus post terras datas blanc: which was applicable to those Rents of his County, which were answered in fine Silver reduced to the test by combustion, or with an allowance of 12*d.* in the Pound in compensation of it.

Firma Comitatus numero, was his Firme for those Rents of his County which were onely answered in Money numbred, without reducing them to their fineness by Combustion, or any satisfaction for it it: But of this more fully in the ensuing Chapter.

I have before mentioned that when any Firme was reserved or answered *blanc*, the Money was to be melted and answered in fine Silver, or at least to Silver allayed to right and finest Sterling; or else he was to redeem himself from that trouble by payment of 12*d.* in the Pound: So that that Person upon whom there was reserved 5*l. blanc* was to pay 5*l.* 5*s.* if he would not have his Money melted down and made good in fine Silver (or at least in true Sterling.) And this appears to be true by infinite Records: Take two or three for instance.

In compoto cum Northampton, 21 H. 3. *Summa totalis* 102l. 3s. 7d. *de qua* 4l. 9s. 4d. blanc, *quæ sunt extensæ ad* 4l. 13s. 9d. *subtrahuntur ad perficiendum corpus Comitatus & remanet* 97l. 13s. 10d. *de quibus respondet de proficuo in magno Rotulo.*

Clauf. 13. H. 3. *m.* 2. *Sciatis quod perdonavimus dilectæ Sorori nostræ* A. *Comitissæ* Pembroc *centum triginta*

ginta & quinque Libras blanc, *quæ extenſæ ſunt ad centum quadraginta & unum Libras, & quindecim Solidos.*

In Compoto Bedf. *&* Bucks, 13 *E.* 3 Nic. Paſſelew *de* 18*l.* 4*s.* 4*d. numero pro* 17*l.* 7*s. blanc.*

In all theſe the proportion riſeth very near, bating the ſmall fragments in Pence, that every Pound *blanc* anſwered one Shilling over, to reduce it to its value.

And hence it is that at this day the ancient Firmors of Cities, as *London, &c.* which were commonly reſerved *blanc*, do pay the ſame in Sterling Money, and one Shilling for every pound over: As if 100*l. blanc* be reſerved, there is anſwered at this day in the Receipt 105*l.* which, as before, makes me ſuppoſe that *blanc* Firme, or *dealbata Firma*, was in truth when it was reduced to fine Silver, and not barely Sterling: for this advance of 12*d.* in the Pound upon ſuch *blanc* Firmes is ſtill anſwered though paid in Sterling.

CHAP.

CHAP. IV.

Concerning the manner of answering the King's Firmes anciently.

IN ancient times, *viz.* about the time of *William* the firſt and *Henry* the ſecond, the reſervation of the King's Firmes and Rents were ſo many Pounds or Shillings, &c. in Money, and they were anſwered *numero*, or *in Pecuniis numeratis*, untill afterward for the avoiding of corrupt Money, they were reſerved in *blanc* or white Money, which, as before is obſerved, was intended either of pure Silver, (or at leaſt Silver reduced to the Allay of Sterling) and then whitened or blanched, as is uſed in the Mint to this day, for all Sterling Money: I ſhall not much contend whether it were the one or the other, but for the moſt part in this Diſcourſe I ſhall ſuppoſe it fine Silver.

But

But although Firmes were reserved in Money, as the best and commonest measures of values, yet it appears by *Tilburiensis, Lib.* 1. *Cap. A quibus & ad quid instituta fuit Argenti examinatio*; that it was in those ancient times of King *W*. 2. and *H*.1. usually practised that those Firmes should, according to their values be answered in Cattle, Corn and other provisions; which perchance in its first institution might be a convenience to the King, to have his Family furnished with provisions *in specie*, and to the Country, among whom Money was not then very plentifull, and they could better answer their Rents in Provisions.

And to the end that an equation might be made between the Rents reserved in Money and the Provision delivered by the Tenants in lieu thereof, the same *Tilburiensis* tells us, there were certain prices and rates set upon provisions, that the Tenant might know what to pay, and the King's Officers might know what to receive. As for Wheat for

100 men 12*d.* for a fat Ox 12*d. &c.* which it seems were dilivered to the hands of the Sheriff who, if he firmed the County, might retain it to his own use; but if he firmed it not he accompted to the King, for these Provisions or their values, as he did for other rates of the County collected by him.

But as for Cities and Franchises that were granted out to Firme, because they had not Provisions of this nature to answer, they paid their Rents in Money.

Thus, it seems, the King's Firmes of Rents of his Firmors and Tenants in the Country were answered in the time of King *William* the first and *William* his son. But in the time of *H.* 1. the Tenants were weary of answering their Rents in provisions, and the King's foreign occasions called rather for a supply of Money, and so the Rents were answered by the Tenants as formerly in Money according to the tenour of their reservations, and the delivery of Victual and other Provisions in lieu thereof ceased. CHAP.

CHAP. V.

Concerning the manner of collecting the King's Revenues of the County, and the several kinds of them with their several Titles.

THE Sheriff of the County had a double Office: 1. As a Minister of Justice under the King for the preservation of Peace, and Writs issuing from the King's Courts. 2. As the King's Bayliff of his Revenues arising in the County, which was of two kinds.

1. The improving and letting, and sometimes stocking of the King's Demesnes, and such Lands as were seized into the King's hands (other than such as belonged to the Escheator, as Wardships and Escheats.) And hence it is that there are upon the accompts, especially of *Bucking-*
D *ham*

ham and *Bedford*, allowances made to the Sheriff of that County *ut* ..... *Comitatus.*

2. The second part of his Office was in collecting of the King's Rents of his County, which sometimes he did as *Custos* or Bayly; sometimes *ut Firmarius, viz.* he took the Rents to his own use, and answered the King a certain Firme or Rent at his own peril, whereof more in the ensuing Discourse. Now concerning the kinds of the King's Revenues arising in the several Counties, we are to take notice that they were of two kinds, *viz.* Annual or Casual.

The Annual Revenue was again of two kinds, *viz.* Fixed and Certain, or Casual and Uncertain.

The Annual, Fixed and Certain Revenue of the Counties were of these kinds.

1. The King's Demesnes that were in his own hands, or let at Rack rents to Tenants, whereof I have before spoken, and they make

not

not much for that purpose I aim at.

2. Firmes, which were of two kinds, *viz.* Grofs Firmes which were charged upon particular perfons, or Cities, or Towns, and fo charged in the great Roll; as thus, *Philippus d'Aura debet 2 Marc. de reditu unius virgate terre.* And thefe were thus charged upon thefe two reafons: 1. Either becaufe they were never parcel of the Sheriffs Firme of this County, *(de quo infra,)* but great Firmes written out to the Sheriff to be anfwered by the perfons upon whom they were charged. 2. Or elfe they were fuch as happened to be referved after the Firme of the County was reduced to certainty and anfwered by the Sheriffs. Or elfe, Secondly, they were fmall rents commonly called Vicontiel Rents; the Particulars whereof we fhall enumerate under their feveral heads in due time.

3 Common Fines, at firft impofed upon Townfhips, upon feveral occafions; as for *Bon pleder*, for Suit and Ward, for excufe of attending

the Sheriffs turn: and thefe grew in procefs of time to be fixed and fetled Revenues. And thefe again were of two Sorts; fuch as came within the Title of *Firma Comitatus*, and were written out under that general head, *viz. fub nomine Vicecomitis*: And fome again were written to the Sheriff in the particular charge of fuch and fuch Townfhips and Lands, and fo charged upon the Towns by the exprefs words of the procefs.

4. Arrentations of Affarts and Purpreftures in Wafts and Forefts fet by Juftices in *Eyre*, which for the moft part were written out in charge againft the particular Lands upon which they were charged: and fome perchance were demanded in a grofs Summ, among other fmall Rents *fub nomine Vicecomitis*.

5. *Crementum Comitatus*, or *Firma de cremento Comitatus*; which were fome improvements of the King's Rents above the ancient Vicontiel Rents, for which the Sheriff anfwered under the title of *Firma Comi-*

Comitatus. And this *Crementum Comitatus* or the several small advances of the old Vicontiel Rents, were answered under the title of *Crementum Comitatus*, or *Firma de cremento Comitatus*. But those kinds of Firmes *de cremento* are onely found in the Counties of *Bedford, Bucks, Norfolk, Suffolk, Warwick, Leicester, Wigorn* and *Gloucester*: Certain other Summs annually charged in gross upon the Sheriff for certain other small or minute Rents under several titles in several Counties; as, *De Cornagio, de Wardis, Castle de Firma, Purprest & Escaet de diversis Firmis, de minutis particulis, Serjancia de tr̄is assert infra divers forest:* all which were charged in gross Summs upon the Sheriff, and *sub nomine Vic.* without expressing any particulars, or upon whom they were charged, which because they were not common to all Countries, but varied according to the various usage of several Counties, I shall not at large handle, but shall content my self with the enquiry

quiry into those that were the common charges of the Sheriffs of every several County, *viz.* the *Corpus Comitàtus*, and the *Proficua Comitatus*.

The Vicontiel Rents that made up the Sheriffs Firme of the Body of the County, came under various Titles and Denominations in several Counties, *viz.*

1. *Reditus Assize in* Cumberland, Hertford, Surry.
2. *Firme & feodi Firme in* Cumberland, Northumberland, Nottingham, Stafford.
3. *Firma antiqua in* Huntington.
4. *Albe Firme in* Norf. & Suff.
5. *Blanch Firmes in* Ebor', & Suff.
6. *Blanc Rents in* Kent.
7. *Albus Cervus in* Dorset.
8. *Auxilium Vicecom' in* Cant', Cumbr', Essex, Hunt', Leic', North', Sussex, Warw', Wilts.
9. *Auxilium ad Turcum Vicecom' in* Devon.
10. *Hidage in* Berks, Bedf. Bucks, Oxon.

11. *Presta-*

Sheriffs Accompts. 39

11. *Preſtatio pro pulchre placitando in* Bedf', Bucks.
12. *Secta & Warda in* Bedf', Bucks.
13. *Viſus Franci plegii in* Bedf', Bucks, Cant', Hunt', Eſſex, Hertford, North'ton, Somerſet, South'ton, Stafford.
14. *Certitudines in* Berks, Heref', Rutland.
15. *Certi reditus in* Lincoln, Leiceſter, Somerſet, South'ton, Warwick & Wilts.
16. *Certi reditus ad communem finem in* Derby, Nottingham.
17. *Reditus pro Warda Caſtri in* Cant', Northum', Oxon, Norf', & Suff'.
18. *Reditus ad Turnum Hundredi in* Dorſet.
19. *Finis antiquus in* Eſſex.
20. *Finis pro ſecta Curie relaxand' in* Berks & Oxon.
21. *Communes fines in* Glouc', Heref', Hertf', Surry, Suffolc, Salop.
22. *Fines Aldermannorum in* Suſſex.

23. *Turnum Vicecom'* in Essex & Hertf'.
24. *Secta Burg. & Vill.* in Cant'.
25. *Suit Silver* in Staff'.
26. *Hundred Silver* in Norf'.
27. *Faith Silver* in Staff'.
28. *Pannel Silver* in Norf'.
29. *Ward Silver* in Essex.
30. *Certum lete cum Capitag'* in Norf'.
31. *Leet fee in* Suff'.
32. *Soken fees in* Suff'.
33. *Mott fee in* Salop.

These are the general Titles of those Vicontiel Rents that usually came under the Title of *Firma Comitatus*, which were written generally *sub Nomine Vicecom'*, without expressions of the particulars: But the Sheriff that had a particular Roll of these Vicontiel Rents, delivered in that Roll many times upon his Accompts, though not written especially in charge under those names, or in particular by the Summons of the Pipe: And thus much concerning the certain Annual Revenue. 2. The

2. The uncertain Annual Revenue was the *Proficuum Comitatus*, which in ancient times when most of the Law-suits were transacted in the Counties and Hundred-Court, was a considerable Revenue. But since that time, *viz.* about the beginning of *E.* 1. when much of that business was transacted at the great Courts, this profit of the County sunk to very little. And in my enquiry touching this part of the Revenue, I shall First set down what it was not: Secondly, I shall set down what it was, and how it did arise.

1. Touching the former of these what it was not; I say, most clearly it was not that profit which is now the onely considerable profit of the Sheriffs employments, *viz.* the Fees and Perquisites for the execution of Writs, and Process and Execution issuing out of the King's Courts. For,

1. Untill the Stat. of 23 *H.*6.*c.*10. there were no Fees at all by Law due for any execution of Process or

Warrants

Warrants for the same. Till the Stat. of 29 *El.* 2. there were no Fees allowed by Law for levying of Debts or Damages: But by the express provision of the Stat. of *Westminster* the first, the Sheriff was bound to execute the King's Process without any Fee, which is no other but a declaration of the Common Law.

2. In no Viscontil Schedule or Accompt of the County that ever I could see or hear of, is there any Accompt for Fees for execution of Process, or any mention thereof.

3. If the Sheriff did in those elder times take any Fees for execution of Writs, there was no colour of reason that he should accompt for that: and if he did take more than a reasonable recompence for his pains, it was more than could be justified, and not at all due to the King.

II. But now, as to the Second enquiry, what this *Proficuum Comitatus* was: And it seems very plain that it was made up principally by these

these particulars, as most evidently appears by divers accompts of Sheriffs in ancient times, when they accompted *ut Custodes* or *Ballivi*, not *ut Firmarii, viz.*

1. The Fines, Issues and Amercements, and other Profits of the County-Courts, which in those ancient times were very considerable, for it held Plea in all Writs that were Vicontiel, directed immediately to the Sheriff out of the Chancery, *viz.* by Justices; and many times not onely personal Suits were removed thither out of inferiour Court-Barons and Hundred-Courts, but also Pleas Real, *viz.* Writs of Right; and in ancient time many real Actions, especially Writs of Right were determined in the County. And therefore it is frequent in the old Schedules of *Proficua Comitatus*, especially in *Yorkshire* in the times of *R.* 1. and King *John*, such as these, *viz.* De J. S. *pro licentia concordandi demimark.* De J. S. *pro Warrantia Essonii* 2 s. and sometimes a Mark *pro mi'a Comitatus*, sometimes

times 10*s. quia retraxit se, Demi-mark. De pretio bonorum per dif-tringas demimark. Pro transgressio-ne 2s. Pro falso clamore demi-mark,* &c.

So that it appears in the accompt of 20 *Johannis Regis,* the profits of the bare County-Court of *York* for one half year amounted to 31 *li.* which is more than 100*l.* in a just estimate at this day.

2. The Profits of the Sheriffs Turns, or the Sheriffs Leets, which had Conusance of matter Criminal, as his County-Court was for matters Civil: and the Profit consisted,

1. In Amercements of Sutors that made default.

2. In the Fines and Amercements of such as were convict of offences inquirable in the turn; as Nusances, Bloudshed, Assize of Bread and Beer, *&c.* and these arose usually to a considerable Summ yearly.

3. The Profits of the Hundred-Courts and Wappentake-Courts; the Profits whereof consisted in the Fines, Amercements and other Perqui-

Perquisites of the Hundred-Court, which the Sheriff sometimes took in kind; sometimes he let it to Firme. These Baylywicks of these Hundreds, and with them the Profits and Perquisites of Courts were sometimes let to Firme by the King, and in such cases the Sheriff accompted *Proficua Ballivatus*, which oftentimes arose to very considerable Summs. In the time of *H.* 3. the Firmes of the Baylywicks of the Hundreds in *Yorkshire*, beside *Stancliff* and *Strafford*, were let for 100*l*. 6*s*. 8*d*. *per annum*, which was then a considerable Summ, and amounts now in Sterling Money to thrice as much. But as the business and jurisdiction of the Hundred-Courts sunk gradually in their employment, (whereby the Perquisites now do but little surmount the charge of keeping them) so now by the Stat. of 23 *H*. 6. *cap*. 10. the Sheriff is restrained from letting the Baylywick to Firme; and most of the Hundreds, at least in many Counties, are disjoined from the County and

and granted out, some in Fee-farm, and some otherwise, though there have been frequent attempts of rejoining them to the Sheriffs by acts of Resumption.

And these are the Profits that made up the *Proficuum Comitatus*, for which the Sheriff most commonly in ancient time answered as *Firmarius* at a certain Rent, though sometimes he accompted for it as *Custos* or *Ballivus* as shall be shewn. And I know no other Perquisite that made up the *Proficuum Comitatus* but what is above mentioned; onely in *Northumberland* there were some Castle gard-Rents that were in truth Vicontiel Rents, and in their propriety and nature belonged to the *Corpus Comitatus*, which yet by constant usage were usually answered among the *Proficua Comitatus*. And thus far concerning the annual Revenue of the County, both Certain and Uncertain, chargeable upon the Sheriffs collection.

2. The Revenue Casual consisted of many Particles under various Heads

Heads or Titles, *viz.* Debts drawn into the Pipe, and thence written out unto the Sheriff. Fines voluntary or compulsary. Seisures of Lands and Compositions, &c. they may be reduced under these three Heads at this day.

1. The Debts written out to the Sheriff from the several Offices, *viz.* the two Remembrancers, Clerk of the Pipe, &c.

2. The Summons of the Green Wax, written to the Sheriff with the Estreats from the Treasurer's Remembrancers.

3. The foreign Accompt, or Seisures of Lands for Debts or Forfeitures.

As touching escheated Lands and Wardships they came under the Escheator's charge, and the Profits thereof rarely answered by the Sheriff, unless for some few ancient Escheats.

CHAP.

CHAP. VI.

Concerning the manner how the Annual Revenue of the County was usually answered in the ancient times untill 10 E. 1.

Having shewed what the Annual Profits of the County consisted of, I shall now descend to the manner how it was anciently answered. The Sheriff, as hath been shewn was the King's Bayly for the collecting of the King's Revenue: And touching the manner of his collecting and answering them, and therein principally concerning those two great parts of the Annual Revenue, *viz.* the *Corpus Comitatus,* or when it was in Firme, the *Firma corporis Comitatus*: And the *Proficuum Comitatus,* and when it was in Firme, the *Firma de proficuo Comitatus*; both which shall be hereafter

hereafter more fully explained.

These Profits were anciently, and are to this day, answered at two Terms in the year, *viz.* Michaelmas and Easter.

But to enable the more effectual levying of them, there always issued to the Sheriff before Easter and Michaelmas, out of the Exchequer a Writ called the Summons of the Pipe, which had annexed to it the charge or Summs for which the Sheriff was answerable, *viz.* those which were charged upon himself *sub nomine Vicecomitis*, and those which are charged upon others. The Form of the Writ is recorded in the black Book of the Exchequer, *Lib. 2. cap. Qualiter fient Summonitiones*; which continue to this day, *viz. Rex Vic' Ebor' Salutem. Vide sicut teipsum & omnia tua diligas quod sis ad Scaccarium nostrum* Westm' *in Cro' Sancti Michaelis, vel in Cro' Clausi* Paschæ, *& habeas ibi quicquid debes de vetere firma vel nova: Et nominatim hæc debita subscripta.* And then the whole charge is inserted which
common-

monly began with these annual Revenues, *viz.*

De Corpore Comitatus
   (or if it were in Firme)
De Firma de Corpore Com. 100 bl.
De Numero Comitatus 10
De Proficuo Comitatus
   (or if in Firme)
De Firma de proficuo Com. 50

And then the Summ in gross charged upon the Sheriff for divers small Rents, and then afterwards all those Firmes that were charged upon particular persons *seriatim* and in order.

And according to the order wherein they were written out to the Sheriff, accordingly in effect were the Accompts passed, and the Entries made thereof in the great Roll of the Pipe, onely the particulars in the Writ was their charge of the Sheriff, unto which he was to give his answer upon his Accompt, and then there are entred his discharges.

And

And this Firme continues there to this day, with such alterations as are hereafter mentioned: and therefore the Ordinance or Statute *in Libro Rubro Scaccarii, fol.* 242. made in 54 *H.* 3. is nothing else but the stable and fixed method for writing the great Roll, observed both before and since that day.

Primò, Scribatur Corpus Comitatus, deinde Eleemosyne constitute, & Liberationes & Bri'a prisci Vicecom' sicut semper fuit consuetum. Deinde oneretur Vic' de Firmis pro proficuo Comitatus vel de proficuis: Deinde scribantur omnes Firme tam majores quam minores, &c.

And although the certain *Debet* of the Sheriff could not be known before the finishing of his Accompt, because it could not be known what he levied, and what not; and what he had paid, and what not; (which Accompt was not untill the end of his year) yet it seems there was anciently an estimate what this constant charge of the annual Revenue amounted unto, and what the constant

stant allowances amounted unto, according to a *medium*, or possibly according to those Firmes and gross Summs which were charged immediately upon the Sheriff *sub nomine Vicecomitis*; and these Summs were paid into the Exchequer at the return of the Writ of Summons of the Pipe, and they were, and are to this day called *Profre Vicecom'*, or the Sheriffs Proffers. And by the Statute of 51 *H*. 3. called *Statutum de Scaccario*, those proffers are appointed to be paid on the morrow of St. *Michael*, and the morrow *post Clausum Paschæ*; and the payment of these proffers are continued to this day: But although they are paid, yet if upon the conclusion of the Sheriffs Accompt, and after the allowances and discharges had by him, it appears that he be in surplusage, or that he is charged with more than indeed he could receive, he hath sometimes, and for the most part, all his proffers paid or allowed to him again: and so indeed it is but a mock-payment, a payment kept

kept on foot to maintain the old method of his Accompt, but is in effect but so much Money lent, for he hath it (and justly enough) allowed to him back again: the reason and justice whereof shall be shewn hereafter. And now to return again from whence we digressed, I shall now search out the meaning of these Firmes, *Corpus Comitatus bl.* and *Numerus Comitatus*, and *Firma de Corpore Comitatus*, and *Proficua Comitatus*, and *Firma de proficuo Comitatus*, I mean as they relate to the Sheriffs Accompt for what the things were is sufficiently discovered before.

Therefore as to the *Corpus Comitatus*, I have already shewn in the precedent Chapter, what it consisted of, *viz.* the Vicontiel Rents of the County; and they consisted of two sorts of payment, *viz.* those that were answered in *blanch* Money, and those that were answered in Money numbred. And this ordinarily made two titles of the *Cor-*

pus Comitatus in most Counties, *viz.* where there were Firmes of these differing natures, and they are then thus noted, *viz.*

De Corpore Comitatus   100*l*. bl.
De Numero Comitatus   50

And they were written out thus generally, without expressing the several Vicontiel Rents, but onely the gross Summs what they amounted to *blanc*, and what they amounted to *numero*, or *de numero Comitatus*. And the Sheriff upon his Accompt was used to bring in a Vicontiel Roll, containing these particular Vicontiel Rents, what they were and what he had levied.

By this it appears that in the first constitution of this Vicontiel Accompt the Sheriff accompted for these Rents as Bayly or *Custos*, and answered what he levied though they were written out, and stood upon the great Roll all in a lump, and when the Sheriff accompted thus, he accompted as *Custos* or Bayly.

But

But in procefs of time (but that time very ancient) the Sheriff for the time being took the *Corpus Comitatus* or Vicontiel Rents to Firme, which Firme for the moft part amounted to very near the entire quantity of the Vicontiel Rents. And this Firme in many Counties was very ancient, for we find them mentioned in the Pipe-rolls of the time of King *John* and *R. 1.*

And by this means the Sheriff was to anfwer at his peril his Firme, for it became his own debt, and he was to gather up the Vicontiel Rents to his own ufe to make himfelf a Saver.

She Sheriffs Commiffion hereupon was with the refervation of the Firme, and although we have not memorials of all thofe refervations, yet of fome we have.

Inter Communia of 19 *E. 1.* Bedf. Bucks, *Rex* 16. *Jan. Anno* 19. *Commifit* Will. Turvil *Com'* Bedf. *&* Bucks *cum pertinent' cuftodiend' quamdiu Regi placuerit reddendo inde per annum quantum* Johannes Palam

Iam *nuper Vicecomes eorundem reddere confuevit.*

And by little and little this grew into a ufage, the fucceeding Sheriff anfwering the Firme of the County, and of the Profits of the County as his predeceffor had done: whereby the *Firma Comitatus* and the *Firma de proficuis Comitatus* became as fetled Firmes charged upon the Sheriff though there were no exprefs refervation of it upon his patent or Commiffion of Sheriff.

And becaufe thefe Firmes were in their firft refervation proportioned to the value and nature of thofe Rents, which now the Sheriff had, as before the King had them, *in fpecie*; hence the Sheriffs Firme of the County or Body of the County as it was proportionable to the fame, anfwered for the Vicontiel Rents; fo it was proportioned to their nature, *viz.* becaufe fome of the Vicontiel Rents were in *blanc* Money, the Sheriffs Firme correfponding to that was anfwered in *blanc* Money: and fome of thofe rents being anfwered swered *numero*, the Sheriffs Firme corresponding thereto was answered *numero*.

And by this Accompt the charge both upon the Summons of the Pipe and upon the great Roll was altered *viz.* whereas the former Style of the charge was *De corpore Comitatus blanc & numero*, now it was changed, *viz.*

De Firma de corpore Com' 100*l.* bl.
De numero Comitatus   40

Ad thus the manner of the charge stood for the times of *H.* 3. and *E.* 1. and for some time before, at least in some Counties: and so it continues to this day with such alterations as shall be shewn.

And as the *Corpus Comitatus* thus by usage grew a Firme, or Rent charged upon the Sheriff, so also did the *Crementum Comitatus*, in those Counties where such *Crementa* was answered, *viz.*

De

De Firma Comitatus   100*l*.
De numero Comitatus   40
De Cremento Comitatus   10

All being governed by the word *Firma*: For, as I have said, a long letting of these Vicontiels to Firme, had brought them to be a setled charge, charged upon, and answered by the Sheriff; and he gathered up the Vicontiels to his own use, to make himself a Saver, and to make good his Firme. And thus much concerning the answering and altering of the charges of the Vicontiels, or the *Corpus Comitatus* both before and after it was in Firme.

2. As concerning the *Proficuum Comitatus*; the proceeding was much the same as that concerning the *Corpus Comitatus*.

In the ancienter times, when the *Proficua Comitatus* was at all answered by the Sheriff, it was answered by him, as *Custos* or Bayly upon Accompt

Sheriffs Accompts. 59

Accompt: Though in some ancient Pipe-rolls, for some Counties we find no distinct mention of it; as in the Pipe-roll of 19 *R*. 1. *Glouc.* Herbertus *reddit compotum de* 372*l*. 14*s*. 6*d*. bl. *de Firma Comitatus.* The like, *ibid.* 13 Johannis. But very frequently afterwards the Sheriffs, when they had the *Corpus Comitatus*, or the Certain Annual Revenues under a Firme, yet answered the *Proficua Comitatus* as *Custos* or Bayly: for instance, *Pipe-roll* 9 *R*. 1. Bedf. & Bucks, Simon *de Bello campo reddit compotum de* 369*l*. 19*s*. 11*d*. bl. *Et de* 79*l*. 8*s*. 1*d*. *numero, de Firma Comita'*, without mentioning the *Proficua Comitatus.*

But in the Pipe-roll 25 *H*. 3. Bedf. & Bucks, Paulinus Pejor, *ut Firmarius reddit compotum de* 369*l*. 19*s*. 11*d*. bl. *& de* 108*l*. *numero de Firma Comitatuum.*

Idem Vicecomes reddit compotum de 100 *marc' pro proficuo Comitat.*

And *Anno* 44. H. 3. Alexander Hampden, *ut Firmarius reddit compotum de* 369*l*. 19*s*. 11*d*. bl. *& de* 108*l*.

108*l. numero, de Firma Comitatuum.*

Idem A. *reddit compotum de* 220 *marc' pro proficuo Comitat' ficut continetur in originali.*

And in 51 H. 3. Galfridus Ruſ *ut Firmarius de anno* 50 *reddit compotum de* 369*l.* 19*s.* 11*d.* bl. *& de* 108*l numero de Firma Comitat'.*

Idem Galfridus *reddit compotum de* 180 *marc' pro proficuo Comitatus de anno* 50. *ficut continetur in quodam Rotulo attachiato originali ejufdem anni.*

And in the year following, Edvardus *filius Regis primogenitus,* Barthol. *de Irene Subvicecomes ejus reddit pro eo per breve Regis, compotum de* 369*l.* 19*s.* 11*d.* bl. *&* 108*l. numero de Firma Comitatus hoc anno.*

Idem E. *Vic' non reddit de aliquo proficuo Comitat' quia Rex ei commifit dictos Comitatus refpond' inde per annum de antiqua Firma corporis, ficut continetur in originali anni precedentis.*

And ſo in the great Roll of 50 *H.* 3. Glouc. Reginaldus *de Ale de* 372*l.* 14*s.* 6*d. de Firma Com'.*

Idem

Idem Vicecomes reddit compotum de 80 *marc' pro proficuo Com' & exit' ville & nundinorum & Hundredi de* Wencham *ficut continetur in quodam Rotulo,* &c. and so it continued in the time of *E.* 1.

By which it is evident, 1. That sometime there was nothing at all answered *pro proficuis,* but it was cast into the Firme of the County. 2. That although the body of the County, consisting of a certain yearly Revenue was in Firme, yet oftentimes the *Proficua Comitatus* were not in Firme, but the Sheriff accompted for them *ut Custos,* sometime higher, sometime lower, as the profits arose.

But in procefs of time the *Proficua Comitatus,* at least in some Counties, fell under a Firme, though in some Counties sooner, in some later; and having once begun to be in Firme, the succeeding Sheriff took it as his predecessour left it; and so it became in time a setled Firme, though not exprefsly reserved upon the Patent of every Sheriff.

And

And yet in such cases it was become a setled Firme, by usage and custome; yet when the Sheriff found that his Firme was too great for these profits (which were casual, sometimes more, sometimes less) he was in those elder times admitted to accompt *ut Custos*, without being bound to answer his entire Firme, unless he saw fit. But that was rarely in use after the time of *H*. 4. and accordingly it seems to be intimated in that ordinance of 54 *H*. 3. above mentioned, for writing the great Roll of the Pipe, *viz. de Firmis pro Proficuis, vel de Proficuis*. And this shall suffice for the unriddling of the Sheriffs Accompts till the 10 and 11 *Ed*. 1.

CHAP.

CHAP. VII.

The Second Period of the Sheriffs Accompts, viz. *How they stood from* 10 E. 1. *untill* 34 H. 8.

WE have in the former Chapter seen how the Statute of the Sheriffs Accompts stood in relation to the annual Revenue of the County, whether Certain or Uncertain, and both stand now reduced under a Firme, *viz.*

1. The *Corpus Comitatus* answered under a Firme; partly *blanc*, and partly *numero*.

2. The *Proficua Comitatus* gradually also reduced into a Firme intirely *numero*; but with a liberty for the Sheriff to ease himself of the excess of his Firme above the profits, by submitting to an accompt of these profits as Bayly or *Custos*.

It fell out in process of time that the Kings of *England* granted away many of those Vicontiel Rents, and the Lands upon which some of them were charged, whereby the Sheriff lost much of what was to make up the Firme of his County. And although the Sheriffs, upon shewing thereof upon their Accompts, had an allowance of that which was so granted away, yet it made a trouble and disorder in the Sheriffs Accompts.

And therefore it was necessary to have some provision for the same, but this onely concerned that part of his Firme which was of the *Corpus Comitatus*, or the Firme of the Certain Annual Revenue. Therefore by the Stat. of *Rutland* 10 *E.* 1, this provision is setled.

Quod non scribatur de cetero corpora Comitatum in Rotulis singulis, quin scribantur in quodam Rotulo annuali per se, & legantur singulis annis super compotum Vicecomitis singula, viz. *in singulis Comitatibus, ut sciatur si quid nobis possit accidere*

In

in quocunque Comitatu. Remanent' vero eorundem Comitatuum post terras datas scribatur in Rotulis annualibus & onerentur inde Vicecomites. In quibus quidem remanentibus allocentur liberationes, eleemosyne, &c. Scribantur etiam in eisdem Rotulis annualibus Firme Vicecomitum, proficui Comitatus, firme Serjantiar' & Assartor', Firme Civitatum, Burgorum & Villarum, & alie Firme de quibus est responsum annuatim ad Scaccarium predictum. Scribantur in eisdem omnia debita terminata & omnia grossa debita de quibus spes est quod aliquod inde reddi possit. Item omnia debita quæ videntur esse clara, titulum de novis oblatis. Nihil scribatur in Rotulo Annuali nisi ea de quibus est spes, &c. De Firmis vero mortuis & debitis de quibus non est spes, fiat unus Rotulus, & irrotulentur & legantur singulis annis super Compot' Vicecom' & debita de quibus Vicecomes respondebat scribantur in Rotulo annuali & ibi acquietentur.

F   And

And by this Act thefe alterations were made.

I. the ftate of the yearly Rents which heretofore made up the *Corpus Comitatus* was examined, and it was confidered what parts thereof had been granted out by the King, to the end that the Sheriffs Firme of the body of the County might be abated with refpect to thofe grants; which reduction of the Firme is ftiled *Remanentia Firme poft terras datas.*

II. The old ftile of *Corpus Comitatus* was now put out of the charge, and whereas formerly the Sheriffs charge was *De Firma de corpore Comitatus*, now it was changed, and the charge was *De remanente Firme poft terras datas :* And accordingly it was forthwith altered in the great Roll, onely when thofe remaining Rents that were to make good this *Remanentia Firme,* did confift of Rents *blanc*, or of Rents *numero* onely, it was accordingly ly written, *viz.* in this manner.

De remanente Firme de Com' 100*l*. bl.
De numero Comitatus 50

III. There was to be extracted out of the great Roll the old Rents that made up the *Corpus Comitatus* and the title thereof, and those Firmes that were *Firme mortue* or *obsolete*, illeviable Firmes, and those debts that were desperate, and the great Roll of the Pipe (which was written every year) was to be disburthened of them, and they were to be transcribed into another Roll called an Exannual Roll.

This Exannual Roll to be yearly read to the Sheriff upon his Accompt, to see what might be gotten: and if any thing appeared to be good, then the same to be recharged again upon the great Roll of the Pipe.

IV. But there was no alteration hereby made of the *Firma de Proficuis*: So that by this Act as in relation to the Firmes and Rents of the County thefe things were done. 1. Thofe Firmes or Rents that were wholly granted away, were wholly put out of charge, whether they were affart Rents or Firmes charged upon particular Perfons or Land, or that were within the Sheriffs Firme as Vicontiel Rents. 2. If any Vicontiel Rents that made up the Sheriffs *Firma de corpore Comitatus* were granted out, the Sheriffs Firme was abated in refpect thereof. 3. If there were any Obfolete or Dead Rents, that were either Vicontiel Rents or charged upon particular Lands or Perfons which had not been a long time anfwered, they together with the *Corpus Comitatus* were removed out of the Annual Roll and tranfmitted into the Exannual Roll read yearly to the Sheriff, to fee whether any hope of levying them: but their writing out in charge in the great Roll fufpended till they might be after difcovered to be leviable.

And accordingly prefently after the making of this Act, the Firme

of

Sheriffs Accompts. 69

of the Sheriffs charge in the Summons of the Pipe and the entry thereof upon the great Roll was changed, and this memorial is made upon the Pipe-roll for every County.

Corpus hujus Comitatus non annotatur hic, sed annotatur in quodam Rotulo in quo scribuntur omnia corpora Comitatuum Angliæ *in manu Regis existentia simul cum Firmis mortuis & debitis quasi desperatis quæ debent singulis annis legi & recitari super Compotum Vic' ut sciatur quid inde accidere possit Regi ex quacunque causa que sunt in Thesauro. In quibus etiam continetur quod inde Vicecomites onerentur in compotis suis predictis de remanentibus Firmarum Comitatuum post terras datas. Et quod in eisdem remanentibus allocentur liberationes & Eleemosyne constitute & alie allocationes si quas Vic' habuerint per Br'ia Regis de eorundem exitibus.*

And according to this Act and Memorandum the great Roll was certified: for inftance, before this Act the great Roll for *Gloucefter* did run thus.

J. F. reddit compotum de 372*l.* 13*s.* 6*d.* blanc. *de Firma Comitatus.*

But after this alteration it runs thus.

In the great Roll 12 *E.* 1. Rogerus *de* Lockington *Vicecomes reddit compotum de* 38*l.* 14*s.* 11*d.* blanc. *de remanente Firme Comitatus poft terras datas.*

Idem Vic' reddit compotum de 80 *marc' de Firma pro proficuis Comitatus* (which was the old Firme thereof before 10 *E.* 1.)

So again in the Pipe-roll 10 *E.* 1. which was the Accompt of the year next before the making of this Act the Roll runs thus, *viz.*

Bedf. Bucks, Richardus *de* Gollington *reddit compotum de* 319*l.* 19*s.* 11*d.* bl. *& de* 108*l. numero, de Firma Comitatus. Et reddit compo-*
tum

tum de 180 *marc' de Firma pro proficuo Comitatus ficut* Johannes *de* Chedley *reddere confuevit.* In the Roll next after the making of this Act it runs thus.

Richardus *de* Gollington *Vic' reddit compotum de* 17*l.* 7*s.* bl. *de remanent' Firme Comitatus poft terras datas ficut fupra continetur,* & *de* 108*l. de Firma numero.*

Et Vic' reddit compotum de 100 *marc' de Firma pro proficuis ficut continetur in Rot.* 11 : By which inftances thefe things appear, *viz.*

1. That the *Firma de Proficuis* continued the fame as before : For therein no alteration was made by the Stat. of *Rutland*.

2. That the Title of the *Firma de corpore Comitatus* was changed into the Title *de remanente Firme Comitatus poft terras datas.*

3. That the quantity of the Firmes were reduced to fmaller Summs with refpect to thofe Firmes or Lands charged therewith formerly and fince granted out.

4. That yet the Titles of *Blanc* and

and *Numero* continued or were omitted as the nature of the Vicontiel Rents that remained ungranted were, *viz.* When all the *blanc* Rents were granted out, the Firme *de remanente* was anſwered onely *numero.* Where all the Rents *numero* were granted the Sheriff anſwered his Firme wholly *blanc.* If part of his Rent *blanc* were granted and nothing of thoſe Rents that were anſwered *numero*, he anſwered the remaining part of his Firme *blanc*, and the entire reſidue *numero.* For the Sheriffs Firme of the County before, and *de remanente* now, did anſwer to the quantity, and alſo to the nature or quality of thoſe Vicontiel Rents that he was to receive to make good his Firme.

But abating that one alteration from *Firma corporis Comitatus* to *de remanente Firme,* and the abridging of the Firme as before, and the diſcharging both of the Summons of the Pipe and the great Roll of thoſe charges that were tranſcribed into the Exannual Roll, the

the rest, both of the charge and great Roll continued as before.

But notwithstanding this provision gave some ease to the Sheriffs in relation to those Firmes, yet the charging of them with these Firmes became a matter of continual complaint, for that they were still charged with these Firmes, yet many of the Rents and benefits that should make good their Firmes were sold or became illeviable after *Rot. Parl.* 25 *E.* 3. *n.* 39. *Item pry les Commons que touts Vicounts que sont charge de certain Firmes pur les Counties ou ils sont Vicounts soient discharge de ceo post resceit de lour Baily per cause de Franchises grant Ronne breve soit mand al Treasurer & Barons deschequer quils faient due allowances al chescun Vicount sur le render de lour Accompts en chescun case la ou ils voilent quil soit reasonable.*

And in the same Parliament in 47, the Sheriffs of *Bedf.* and *Bucks* pray to be discharged of the Firmes of the Baylywick of their Hundreds, because those Baylywicks yielded

yielded no profit: they are remitted to the Exchequer, *Rot. Parl.* 45 *E.* 3. *n.* 45. The Sheriffs of *Eſſex* and *Hertford*, pray an eaſe in reſpect of illeviable Firmes charged upon them, and Hundreds and Rents granted from them: anſwered, *Le Roy lour ad ſait grace.*

By the Statute of 1 *H.* 4. *cap.* 11. upon the complaint that the Sheriffs are charged with the ancient Firmes of their County, notwithſtanding that great part of the profits of the ſame be granted to Lords and others: It is enacted that the Sheriffs ſhall accompt in the Exchequer and have an allowance by their Oaths of the iſſues of their Counties.

Rot. Parl. 11 *H.* 4. *n.* 46. *& ſequent'.* The Sheriffs of ſeveral Counties complain that they are charged with ſeveral ancient Firmes which they are not able to levy, *viz. Eſſex* and *Hertf.* with the Firme of the County, and the Firme of the profits of the County: *York* with the Firme of the County *poſt terras datas*

datas. *Devonshire* with the *remanent' Firme Comitatus post terras datas,* the *Firma de Proficuis Comitatus,* and a certain Firme of 100 marks called blanch Firme. *Norfolk* and *Suffolk* with a Firme called *de remanent' Firme post terras datas,* and *Firma de Proficuo Comitatus,* whereof they complain that they cannot levy any thing, and besides the Hundred and Liberties granted out to the diminution of their profit; and pray remedy according to the Stat. of 1 *H.* 4.

They are referred to the King's Council to make such pardon and mitigation as they shall think reasonable.

Rot. Parl. 1 *H.* 5. *n.* 34, 35. The like complaints are made in the behalf of the Sheriffs, and prayed that they may have allowances out of their Firmes upon their oaths according to the Statute of 1 *H.* 4. But they have the like answer as before, *viz.* a reference to the Council.

But *Rot. Parl.* 4 *H.* 5. *n.* 24. and 4 *H.* 5. *cap.* 2. The like petition is received

received, *viz.* that by their oaths they may have an allowance of what the cannot levy out of those great Firmes that are charged *sub nomine Vic'*, *viz.* Firmes of their Counties, *blanc* Firmes *de novo incremento*, &c. But inftead of redrefs they loft that benefit which the Statute of 1. *H.* 4. had before afforded them. And it is directly enacted that the Sheriffs fhall have allowances by their oath of things cafual, which lye not in Firme or annual demand: But of thofe things which lye in Firme annual, or demand annual, they be charged as Sheriffs in aforetime had been charged. And thus ftood the bufinefs of the Sheriffs Firmes untill the Statute of 34 *H.* 8. which is the next Period.

CHAP.

CHAP. VIII.

Touching the State of the Sheriffs Firmes from the Statute of 34 H. 8. *till the fourteenth year of the Reign of King* Charles 1. *which is the Second Period.*

WE have seen in the former Chapter how the case stood with the Sheriffs Firme after the Statute of *Rutland*, and how the Statute of 4 *H.* 5. *cap.* 2. bound the Firmes charged upon the Sheriffs, closer upon them than for some years before: and so they continued till the making of the Statute of 34 *H.* 8. *cap.* 16.

This Statute recites those several Firmes charged to the Sheriff *sub nomine Vicecomitis*, viz. *de remanent' Firme post terras datas: Firma de Proficuo Comitatus*, and those other minute Firmes demanded

ded *sub nomine Vicecomitis*. And many of these particular small Rents that made up these Firmes charged upon the Sheriffs are lost or not leviable, or extinguished by Attainders and Dissolutions of Monasteries, and yet the Sheriffs continue charged with their Firmes as formerly. It enacts,

1. That all Sheriffs that have no Tallies of Record shall upon their days of prefixion deliver in Rolls or Schedules of Parchment containing the particular Summs of Money which he hath or might have levied as parcel of the said ancient Firmes, naming the Person and Lands of which they are to be levied.

2. That after such Schedules delivered the Court shall have power to allow and make deductions in the said Sheriffs Firmes of all such Summs of Moneys as the Firmes shall be more than the Summs in such Schedules shall amount unto.

3. And the Court shall proceed to the recovery of such Summs belonging

longing to the said Firmes as are omitted in such Schedules.

4. That the Sheriff have allowance and discharge of all such illeviable Summs as are written to him in process.

5. That the Sheriff have allowance for entertainment of Justices, &c.

But this was but a temporary Act, and discontinued at the next Parliament. But a farther Act was after made for the ease of the Sheriff, especially in relation to those Firmes; *viz.* 2 and 3 *E.* 6. *cap.* 4. By this it is enacted,

1. That the Sheriff shall have such allowances and Tallies of reward as they had before the Act of 34 *H.* 8. or may accompt according to the Act at their election.

2. That they that accompt and take no Tally of Record shall be treated in the Exchequer as though the Act of 34 *H.* 8. were in force.

3. That those that have no Tallies of reward shall have allowance of the Diet of the Justices, &c.

4. That

4. That all such Sheriffs as take no tallies of reward shall be discharged of all Firmes, Goods, Chattels, Profits, Casualties, &c. as they cannot levy or come by.

5. That all that have Tallies of Reward shall be discharged of all Firmes and Summs of Money that they cannot levy, except Vicontiels with which they are to remain chargeable as before the making of the former Act.

6. That Sheriffs shall have allowances of such Vicontiels as are extinguished by unity of possession in the Crown by dissolution of Monasteries.

7. That the Sheriff at his day of prefixion when he is sworn to his accompt, shall be sworn to deliver into the Court of Exchequer, Rolls or Schedules of Parchment containing all the particular Summs of Money which he hath levied or might levy of his Vicontiels or other Firmes, mentioning the Persons and Lands of which they are leviable, and the Court to take care for the levying

Sheriffs Accompts. 81

levying of such of the Vicontiels, or Firmes, which are omitted out of the Schedules, for saving the King's rights, and to make out process for the same.

Upon these Acts these things are observable.

I. That those Sheriffs that have Tallies of reward may not discharge themselves of their Vicontiels, *viz.* the *Remanent' Firme post terras datas,* and *Crō Comitatus,* and other small Rents charged *sub nomine Vicecomitis* (if he take his Tally of reward) by oath that he cannot levy it, or all of it.

II. But if such a Sheriff will wave his Tally of reward, he may accompt according to the Statute of 34 *H.* 8. and so discharge himself of his Vicontiels or Firmes thereof as well as other Firmes. And the truth is, I think, anciently there were some Sheriffs that had Tallies

G

lies of reward, *viz. York*, *Northampton, Cumb'land, Hereford,* &c.

But since the making of this Act they have waved them, accounting it more beneficial to take the benefit of those Statutes upon their accompt; than to take their Tallies of reward. So that now all Sheriffs have an equal benefit of the Statutes of 34 *H.* 8. and 2 and 3 *E.* 6.

III. But those Sheriffs that had no Tallies of reward might discharge themselves of their Vicontiels and Firmes *de remanente Comitatus*, as well as other things that they could not levy.

IV. That all Sheriffs, as well those that had or had not Tallies of reward might discharge themselves of the casual charges, or their annual uncertain charges; and consequently might, and most ordinarily after this Statute did discharge themselves of the entire Firme *de proficuis Comitatus*, in case the profits of their

their Counties did not furmount the charge that attended them. And by this means fince the making of this Statute, thofe Sheriffs that were charged with the *Firma de proficuis* rarely if at all anfwered any thing for it, becaufe they have always afcertained the Court that there were no fuch profits beyond the charge in collecting them: or that the charge of keeping the County-Court, the Turns, the Hundred-Courts, which were the things that made up the *Firma de proficuis*, furmounted the benefit.

V. And this making appear was no other than the oath of the Sheriff, that he could not levy this or that Rent, parcell of his Vicontiels, or that there were no *Proficua Comitatus*, &c. And this oath of the Sheriff hath always been the Warrant to difcharge him of all or any part of his Firmes. By which means it hath moft ordinarily come to pafs that although the Sheriff hath paid in his profers at Easter and Michaelmas, yet when he comes upon his accompt he doth by his oath discharge himself of all his *Firma de remanente Comitatus*, and thereby most times the King becomes Debtor to the Sheriff for those Moneys which he received as profers, or Moneys due by the Sheriff upon his Firme.

And it is but reason; for the Statute gives him that just benefit to discharge himself by his oath of what he cannot levy or receive.

And yet though the Sheriffs have constantly by their oath discharged themselves of the entire Firme *de Proficuis Comitatus*, and of a great part of their other Firmes of the Viconticls, or *Remanent' Firme*, and other Rents charged upon them in gross Summs, by swearing the illeviableness of some of those Viconticls which make up those *Remanent' Firme Comitatus* and gross Summs, yet constantly after this Act and until the year of our Lord 1650

Sheriffs Accompts. 85

1650 the entire Firmes, *viz.* the entire Firme of the *Remanent' post terras datas,* and the entire Firme *de proficuis Comitatus,* were constantly written out in charge to the Sheriff upon the Summons of the Pipe, and entirely charged upon the great Roll, as they had ever been since the Statute of *Rutland,* and in the very same manner, though in truth it was for the most part but an idle piece of formality; for the Sheriffs constantly swear it off by virtue of the Statute. And thus by these Statutes the Sheriff had ease by his oath from that part and those parts of his Firmes that he sweared he could not levy.

But the truth is the Sheriffs have taken that part of the Statute which was for their ease, *viz.* to swear in discharge of their Firmes, but have two much omitted that other part of the Statute that was for the King's advantage, *viz.* the delivery in upon their oaths the Schedules of their Vicontiels: by which omission possibly

G 3

sibly many small, but good, Rates have been lost since the Statute of 2 and 3 *E.* 6. which might have been preserved. Although possibly the far greater part were lost long before, as appears by the complaints of the Sheriffs, in relation to their Firmes, in the Parliament Roll of 11 *H.* 4. above mentioned, And thus the Sheriffs Firmes stood untill the 15th of King *Charles* the first.

CHAP.

CHAP. IX.

The Third Period from the fifteenth year of King Charles *the first untill the year of our Lord* 1650. *And how the Sheriffs Firmes and Accompts stood in that interval.*

BY an order of the Court of Exchequer made the 25th. *Junii,* 15 *Car.* 1^{mi}. upon the complaint of the King's Firmor of decayed Rents it was ordered that the Clerk of the Pipe should cast up and compute, and severally and distinctly put in charge arrearages of decayed Rents and parcells of Rents, that process and commissions might be made forth thereupon by virtue of the order. But this proved uneffectual, for although the same was done accordingly, yet the King received litte advantage thereby, neither did it at all convenience the Sheriff, or alter the charge written out in the Summons of the Pipe, or upon the great Roll. For the Firmes continued still in charge as before, without any alterations: And though somewhat of small consequence was found out, which might help to make good the Sheriffs Firmes in some particulars, yet the same still fell short, and the Sheriffs were still enforced to make use of the advantage of the Statute of 2 *E.* 6. to ease themselves by their oath of illeviable Rents, till the year 1650.

CHAP.

CHAP. X.

The Fourth Period of the Sheriffs Firmes from the year 1650 unto this day, and how they were answered in that interval.

IN the times of the late troubles, *viz.* 6. *Julii*, 1650. there was an order made in the Court of Exchequer touching the Sheriffs Firmes and the Vicontiel Rents, which because it hath set a Rule in this Business, which to this day is observed, I shall here transcribe *verbatim.*

" Whereas the Sheriffs of several
" Counties of *England* stand char-
" ged in the great Roll of the Pipe,
" and have so stood charged anci-
" ently with divers Summs of Mo-
" ney

"ney in grofs, *sub nomine Viceco-*
"*mitis,* under the feveral Titles of
"*de rem' Firm' Com' poſt terras da-*
"*tas : de veteribus Cr̃i Comitatus.*
"*De Firma de proficuo Comitatus.*
"*De Cornagio. De Warda Caſtri.*
"*De Firma perpreſtur' & eſcaet.*
"*De emerſis Firmis. De minutis*
"*particulis. Serjantia de tr̃is Aſ-*
"*ſart' infra diverſas Foreſtas,* and
"the like. And the faid Sheriffs
"yearly, and from year to year,
"have been and ſtill are comman-
"ded by the Summons of the Pipe,
"to levy the ſame as heretofore to
"the uſe of the Crown, ſo now to
"the uſe of the Common-wealth,
"without expreſſing where, of
"whom, for what cauſe, or out of
"what Lands or Tenements the
"ſame are particularly to be levi-
"ed by the faid Sheriffs, or out of
"what particulars the faid Summs
"in grofs do ſo ariſe; in regard
"whereof, and that it hath hereto-
"fore appeared in the time of King
"*H.* 8. upon complaint of the She-
"riffs,

Sheriffs Accompts.

" riffs, that a great part of the par-
" ticular Rents and annual Summs
" of Money, wherewith the said
" Sheriffs do stand charged upon
" their Accompts in gross, had been
" long before that time payable by
" Monasteries, Abbots, Priors, at-
" tainted Persons, and the like,
" whose Estates were come to the
" Crown, and so ought to be dis-
" charged by unity of possession;
" and yet that the said Sheriffs were
" still charged in gross with the
" same, to their great burthen and
" grievance; it was in the 34th
" year of the said late King *H.* 8.
" enacted by Parliament in the
" case of these Sheriffs, and of all
" Sheriffs for the time to come;
" that the said Sheriffs should be
" charged to answer upon their Ac-
" compts yearly such Rents and
" Summs of Money of the natures
" aforesaid onely, as by the parti-
" cular Rentals or Vicontiels, by
" them to be yearly delivered in
" upon oath, they should set forth
" and

"and make appear to be by them
"leviable; and that they should
"be discharged of all the residue
"which they upon their Oaths
"should affirm to be illeviable, by
"virtue of the said Act of Parlia-
"ment, which hath been so con-
"tinued accordingly, ever since.
"Howbeit the Sheriffs have from
"time to time complained, and
"still complain against the writing
"forth of more to be levied and
"answered by them upon their Ac-
"compts, than such Rents and
"Summs of Money onely as ap-
"pears upon the oaths of their
"predecessors, Sheriffs, to be le-
"viable; and that the rest, ap-
"pearing to be illeviable, ought
"to be removed out of their said
"annual Roll, and Commissions
"thereupon to be awarded out of
"the Exchequer, for reviving the
"same according to the true in-
"tention of the said Statute of
"34 *H.* 8. which the now Lord
"chief Baron, and the rest of the
"Barons,

" Barons, taking into their ſerious
" conſideration, and being willing
" and deſirous, ſo far forth as may
" ſtand with the preſervation of
" the due rights of the Common-
" wealth, to give all fitting eaſe
" and ſatisfaction to Sheriffs there-
" in, according to the meaning of
" the ſaid Statute of 34 *H.* 8. and
" according to the Statute of *Rut-*
" *land*, 10 *Ed.* 1. whereby it is
" provided that nothing ſhall be
" written out to the Sheriffs but
" ſuch Firmes and Debts whereof
" there is ſome hope that ſome-
" thing may be levied. And that
" all dead Firmes and deſperate
" Debts are to be removed from
" the annual or great Roll into the
" exannual Roll, and not to be
" written forth in proceſs to the
" Sheriff, but to be inquired of
" to ſee if any thing may be revi-
" ved. Whereupon the ſaid Lord
" chief Baron and the reſt of the
" Barons, calling before them the
" Clerk of the Pipe, with the Se-
" conda-

"condaries, and the reft of the
"sworn Clerks of the said Office,
"and upon debate of the businefs,
"finding it to be a work of great
"difficulty, labour and care, to
"examine and set forth in every
"County, from the Originals and
"Records of such antiquity to be
"compared with later times, the
"particulars which are from hence-
"forth to be written to the Sheriffs
"to levy in certain. And such as are
"for the reasons aforesaid to be re-
"moved out of the said annual Roll
"have neverthelefs in ease of all
"Sheriffs for time to come, with
"respect to the labour and care of
"the Officers and Clerks to be by
"them undergone therein. It is
"this day ordered that the Clerk
"of the Pipe, the Secondaries and
"other sworn Clerks of the said
"Office in their several affignments
"shall in pursuance of the said
"Statute of *Rutland*, and the said
"Statute of 34 *H*. 8. use their best
"endeavour, diligence and care,
"with

"with as much convenient speed as a work of so great labour and consequence may well be performed, fully to explain and set forth, and shall from henceforth fully explain and set forth, in the subsequent annual Roll of this Court, so many of the particular Rents as they find out and discover by any of the Remembrances, Books, Vicontiels of Sheriffs, or other Records of this Court, to have been, and which be appertaining to the making up of every of the said Firmes so charged in gross Summs as aforesaid, and shall therein distinguish which and how much of those particular Rents have been, and are to be yearly answered.

"And so much of the said Firmes as cannot be explained by setting forth the particulars, together with the particulars so set forth and explained, which have been in decay and unanswered by the space of forty years last past, and
"which

"which are become illeviable, shall
"be thereupon removed and con-
"veyed out of the said annual Roll
"and Sheriffs Accompts into the
"exannual Roll of this Court.
"And that Commissions and Pro-
"cess shall be from time to time a-
"warded to regain and recover the
"same, according to the true in-
"tention of the said Statutes.

This Order produced these Effects.

I. Great care was taken to collect and set forth the obscure Rents, and upon what they were charged.

II. The particulars of those Rents and Vicontiels that made up the Sheriffs Firmes formerly, of *Remanent' Firme post terras datas*, and *De Cremento Comitatus*, as also those Rents that were charged upon the Sheriffs in gross Summs, as *De diversis Firmis, De minutis particulis Serjantiarum*, and such other charges

charges in grofs were wholly left out and omitted.

IV. Inſtead thereof ſuch particular Rents and Vicontiels as made up formerly theſe Firmes and groſs charges, or Money of them as could be diſcovered were particularly written out in the Summons of the Pipe, and in the great Roll firſt under the title of ſeveral Hundreds, wherein the Bills lay that were charged or had any Lands charged within them with theſe Vicontiels and the ſeveral Vills under the Titles of theſe Hundreds, and the ſeveral Lands that were charged within thoſe Vills, as far forth as could be diſcovered.

V. Thoſe Vicontiels that were part of thoſe Firmes or groſs charges, and likewiſe ſuch particular Rents charged formerly in the annual Roll in particular, which had not been anſwered in forty years before, were removed out of the
H Summons

Summons of the Pipe and great Roll into the exannual Roll to be put in procefs as they could be difcovered. And thus the form of the charge which had continued ever fince 10 *E.* 1. as to the Firmes and grofs Summs, was too lately changed to the great eafe of the Sheriffs, of the Court and of the People, who were often haraffed by the Sheriffs to make themfelves favers, by levying thefe obfcure incertain and illeviable Summs. And all this without any detriment to the King who indeed before had an appearance of great Firmes and Summs expreffed in the Summons of the Pipe and great Roll, which yet were fworn off too little by the Sheriffs in purfuance of the Statute of 23 *E.* 6.

VI. But befides all this, the *Firma de proficuo Comitatus* was alfo wholly laid afide and put out of the charge of the Summons of the Pipe and the great Roll. It is true there

Sheriffs Accompts. 99

there is no clear warrant for putting the Firme out of charge by that order, for that order seems to extend onely to Rents and Vicontiels, which indeed made up the other in Firmes and gross Summs charged upon the Sheriffs. But this Firme was answered for the profits of Courts and other casual perquisites, and not in respect of any Vicontiel or annual Rent. But yet for all that, the true extent of that order might extend to put that Firme wholly out of charge, since it is apparent that the profits of the Sheriffs Courts whether Hundred-Courts, County-Courts or *time*, do scarce quit the charges of keeping them at this day, nor for a long time past. Neither is the King *de facto* at any loss thereby, for though before this order this Firme was indeed in charge and carried the shew of some benefit to the King, yet it was wholly sworn off by the Sheriffs by virtue of the Statute of 2 and 3 *E.* 6.

Onely it seems reasonable that though the *Firma de proficuis* be put out of charge so that the Sheriff should not be compelled to answer a Firme to that which yields little or no benefit, yet that the Sheriff should be charged to accompt for the *Proficua Comitatus* as Bayly or *Custos* though not as Firmor.

And that therefore there should stand in charge upon him to accompt *de Proficuis*, which is all that I can find considerable to be supplied in that order, or in the present methodizing of the great Roll in relation hereunto. And although this order was made in the late time of trouble, yet it hath obtained and stood in force unto this day.

The late Act of this Parliament intituled *An Act for the preventing of the unnecessary delays of Sheriffs*, &c. hath this Clause sutable to the said order, *viz*.

" And to the end that Sheriffs
" may for the time future be eased
" of

"of the great charge and trouble
"which they heretofore have been
"put to in passing their Accompts
"in the Exchequer, occasioned part-
"ly in regard that divers Summs
"of Money have stood charged
"upon them in gross without ex-
"pressing from what persons, or
"for what cause, or out of what
"Lands and Tenements, the
"same are particularly to be le-
"vied, or out of what particu-
"lars the said Summs in gross do
"arise, whereby it cometh to pass
"that the Sheriffs do still stand
"charged in gross with divers
"Summs of Money which were
"heretofore payable by Abbots,
"Priors, Persons attainted, and
"such other Persons, whose E-
"states are since come to the
"Crown, or are otherwise dis-
"charged or illeviable. And part-
"ly by the Accompt of Seisures,
"or foreign Accompts, and by
"exaction of undue Fees of She-
"riffs upon their opposals. But it
"is

"is enacted, &c. that no Sheriffs
"shall be charged in accompt to
"answer any illeviable Seisure,
"Firme, Rent or Debt, or either
"Seisure, Firme, Rent, Debt or
"other matter or thing whatsoe-
"ver, which was not writ in pro-
"cess to him or them to be levied
"wherein, the persons of whom,
"or the Lands and Tenements out
"of which, together with the cause
"for which the same shall be so levi-
"ed shall be plainly and particu-
"larly expressed, but shall be there-
"of wholly discharged without Pe-
"tition, Plea or other trouble or
"charge whatsoever.

This Act had in effect discharged the old charges in gross, had not this business been before setled by the order of 1650. But by that order the same thing is done and much more, and put into a very good order.

And thus I have done with this intricate Argument touching the Sheriffs

Sheriffs Firmes. And the occasion of my strict enquiry into it was, a difference between the Auditors and the Clerk of the Pipe: upon the whole debate whereof, I found onely these matters.

1. That, in truth, the great occasion of complaint was, that the Clerks of the Pipe used different methods of accompting from the Auditors of the Revenue, the not observance whereof occasioned a mistaken representation by the Auditors that there was a deceit in their Accompts, whereas it appeared to be no such thing: for when both accompted their several ways, the issue was that the Accompts agreed in the conclusion.

2. That the Firme *de proficuo Comitatus* was put out of charge without Warrant, and it was thought by the Auditors, a great and considerable loss to the Crown, supposing that the Fees for execution of Process

cess and Writs were to make up that Firme: but this is sufficiently unriddled before.

3. That there was an allowance to the Sheriff of *Bucks* of a considerable yearly Summ, *ut Apparatori Comitatus:* This indeed ought not to be allowed at this day, the reason thereof ceasing as hath been shewed; and therefore from henceforth that charge is to be disallowed, but the Clerk of the Pipe not greatly blamable herein, because there was an order of the Court in the Queens time for making that allowance: But the reason whereupon that order was made was a mistake and an errour in the Court not in the Clerk that followed the order.

4. That there is no accompt given for the Firmes of Baylywicks as was anciently; which indeed, was parcel of the *Proficuum Comitatus,* as hath been shewed. But the

the truth is, there is no great reason for any such complaint, the Firmes of Baylywicks being taken away by Act of Parliament, and levy disused in most places.

5. That when a Sheriff is in Surplusage they make it good unto him out of any other debt by the Sheriff himself, or any other Sheriff of the same or any other County, without any Warrant from my Lord Treasurer or the Court. And besides that, the other Sheriff is discharged upon the Roll of his Debt, and it doth not appear upon what reason. And indeed, this is a thing fit to be reformed, and that such allowances be not made without Warrant from the Lord Treasurer, or Order of Court, and that an Entry or Memorandum thereof be made upon the Roll of the Debts so discharged. But yet, the truth is, this manner of allowance hath been a long time used, and it is no novelty or late attempt, neither is there any great damage

damage to the King by it, for it is but the payment of one real Debt with another. But howsoever, this is fit to be reformed by order of the Court that the Sheriffs deliver not in the Roll of the Vicontiel as is required by the Statute. And it is true, he ought to doe it or should be sworn thereunto. But the necessity is not now so great, because the particular Rents are now charged upon the great Roll by virtue of the order of 1650, which doth in a great measure supply that defect, and yet the delivery in of the Vicontiel Roll may be fit to be revived.

The most of the rest of the complaints were touching particulars mischarged, or not charged, but the Errours were rather in the Complainers than in the Pipe, and for want of a clear understanding of those intricate and obscure proceedings of the Pipe. And upon a full search of the particulars, I find the Clerks of the Pipe gave very clear satisfaction therein.

Upon

Upon the whole matter of these Accompts, I do observe these Two or Three Observables.

I. That the inconvenience of retaining the old formalities of proceedings, the same terms and words, and very same mood of all things in Accompts, when the nature of things and times requires a change, and accommodation of new forms or expressions as a piece of hurtfull superstition; therefore, although the change of forms of this nature is not to be done rashly and precipitantly, yet when the exigence of things requires it, there must be an accommodation to the present use, understanding and exigence of affairs.

And hence it is that the Accompts of the Auditors of the Revenue are more easily intelligible as being framed to the use and exigence of the times; but the Accompts of the Pipe more mysterious and

and perplexed, to persons unacquainted with them, for till 10 *E*. 1. they kept in all things the precise form of writing their great Roll, as had been used in King *Stephen's* time. And the same form they kept untill 1650, abating the alterations made in 10 *E*. 1. not without great inconvenience to the King's people and Sheriffs.

II. That these small Rents and Vicontiels would be with much more advantage to the King, and be sold off to the several Persons and Townships chargable therewith, than be kept in method of collection, as now they are, unless some more ready collecting of them by the Receivers could be thought upon, provided the Money arising by sale be laid out presently in more certain Revenue: For, 1. They are in respect of their smallness, and dispersedness, and uncertainty of charge and manner of collecting very subject to be lost, as they have

have been commonly from time to time. 2. The charge of collecting and accompting for them by the Sheriff is very great, and the trouble and charge to the people very much more. 3. The cost and trouble to the King in respect of Officers writing and other matters relating thereunto, might be well retrenched thereby. And yet when all is done, it brings a great trouble, and makes a great noise as if it were a Revenue of great moment, and yet by that time the Sheriffs have done swearing of particulars as illeviable, or that they know not where to charge it, it becomes a very pitifull inconsiderable business, and scarce answering the charge of the collecting, accompting and answering it. For it must be observed that although by the order of 1650, the charge is more certain than formerly, yet the Sheriff hath still by the Law the benefit of the Statute of 2 and 3 *E*. 6. even as to those ascertained Rents, and if he cannot find them he is, and ought to to be discharged upon his oath thereof. And accordingly is daily discharged of many of those Rents though rendred much more certain by that order, and the pains and method of the Charge and Accompt, used in pursuance hereof. Whereby in process of time, many, even of these Rents particularly charged by virtue of that order, will be successively lost.

Sed de his curent Superiores.

FINIS.

A TRYAL OF WITCHES,

AT THE

ASSIZES

HELD AT
Bury St. Edmonds for the County of *SUFFOLK*; on the Tenth day of *March*, 1664.

BEFORE

Sir MATTHEW HALE Kt.

THEN

Lord Chief Baron of His Majesties Court of EXCHEQUER.

Taken by a Person then Attending the Court

LONDON,

Printed for *William Shrewsbery* at the Bible in *Duck-Lane.* 1682.

READER.

THis *Tryal of* Witches *hath lain a long time in a private Gentleman's hands in* the Country, *it being given to him by the Perſon that took it in the Court for his own ſatisfaction; but it came lately to my hands, and having peruſed it, I found it a very remarkable thing, and fit to be Publiſh'd; eſpecially in theſe times, wherein things of this nature are ſo much controverted, and that by perſons of much Learning on both ſides. I thought that ſo exact a Relation of this* Tryal *would probably give more ſatisfaction to a great many perſons, by reaſon that it is pure Matter of Fact, and that evidently Demonſtrated; than the Arguments and Reaſons*

To the Reader.

Reasons of other very Learned Men, that probably may not be so Intelligible to all Readers; especially, this being held before a Judge, whom for his Integrity, Learning, and Law, hardly any Age, either before or since could parallel; who not only took a great deal of paines, and spent much time in this Tryal himself; but had the Assistance and Opinion of several other very Eminent and Learned Persons: So that this being the most perfect Narrative of any thing of this Nature hitherto Extant, made me unwilling to deprive the World of the Benefit of it; which is the sole Motive that induced me to Publish it.

Farewel.

A Tryal of Witches.

At the Assizes and General Gaol-delivery, held at Bury St. Edmonds *for the County of Suffolk, the Tenth day of* March, *in the Sixteenth Year of the Reign of our Sovereign Lord King* Charles II. *before* Matthew Hale *Knight, Lord Chief Baron of His Majesties Court of* Exchequer; Rose Cullender *and* Amy Duny, *Widows*, *both of* Leystoff *in the County aforesaid, were severally indicted for Bewitching* Elizabeth *and* Ann Durent, Jane Bocking, Susan Chandler, William Durent, Elizabeth *and* Deborah Pacey: *And the said* Cullender *and* Duny, *being arraigned upon the said Indictments, pleaded* Not Guilty: *And afterwards, upon a long Evidence, were found* Guilty, *and thereupon had Judgment to dye for the same.*

The Evidence whereupon these Persons were convicted of Witchcraft, *stands upon divers particular Circumstances.*

I. THree of the Parties above-named, viz. *Anne Durent, Susan Chandler*

Chandler, and *Elizabeth Pacy* were brought to *Bury* to the Assizes and were in a reasonable good condition: But that Morning they came into the Hall to give Instructions for the drawing of their Bills of Indictments, the Three Persons fell into strange and violent fits, screeking out in a most sad manner, so that they could not in any wise give any Instructions in the Court who were the Cause of their Distemper. And although they did after some certain space recover out of their fits, yet they were every one of them struck Dumb, so that none of them could speak neither at that time, nor during the Assizes until the Conviction of the supposed Witches.

As concerning *William Durent*, being an Infant, his Mother *Dorothy*

A Tryal of Witches.

rothy Durent sworn and examined deposed in open Court, That about the Tenth of *March, Nono Caroli Secundi,* she having a special occasion to go from home, and having none in her House to take care of her said Child (it then sucking) desired *Amy Duny* her Neighbour, to look to her Child during her absence, for which she promised her to give her a Penny: but the said *Dorothy Durent* desired the said *Amy* not to Suckle her Child, and laid a great charge upon her not to do it. Upon which it was asked by the Court, why she did give that direction, she being an old Woman and not capable of giving Suck? It was answered by the said *Dorothy Durent,* that she very well knew that she did not give Suck, but that for some years before, she had gone under the Reputation of a *Witch*, which was one cause made her give her the caution: Another was, That it was customary with old Women, that if they did look after a sucking Child, and nothing would please it but the Breast, they did use to please the Child to give it the Breast, and it did please the Child, but it sucked nothing but Wind, which did the Child hurt. Nevertheless after the departure of this Deponent, the said *Amy* did Suckle the Child: And after the return of the said *Dorothy*, the said *Amy* did acquaint her, *That she had given Suck to the Child* contrary to her command. Whereupon the Deponent was very angry with the said *Amy* for the same; at which the said *Amy* was much discontented, and used many ny high Expressions and Threatning Speeches towards her; telling her, *That she had as good to have done otherwise than to have found fault with her, and so departed out of her House:* And that very Night her Son fell into strange fits of swounding, and was held in such terrible manner, that she was much affrighted therewith, and so continued for divers weeks. And the said Examinant farther said, that she being exceedingly troubled at her Childs Distemper, did go to a certain Person named Doctor *Jacob*, who lived at *Yarmouth*, who had the reputation in the Country, to help children that were Bewitch'd; who advis'd her to hang up the Childs Blanket in the Chimney-corner all day, and at night when she put the Child to Bed, to put it it into the said blanket, and if she found any thing in it, she should not be afraid, but to throw it into the Fire. And this Deponent did according to his direction; and at night when she took down the Blanket with an intent to put her Child therein, there fell out of the same a great Toad, which ran up and down the hearth, and she having a young youth only with her in the House, desired him to catch the Toad, and throw it into the Fire, which the youth did accordingly, and held it there with the Tongs; and as soon as it was in the Fire it made a great and horrible Noise, and after a space there was a flashing in the Fire like Gun-powder, making a noise like the discharge of a Pistol, and thereupon the Toad was no more seen nor heard.

heard. It was asked by the Court, if that after the noise and flashing, there was not the Substance of the Toad to be seen to consume in the fire? And it was answered by the said *Dorothy Durent*, that after the flashing and noise, there was no more seen than if there had been none there. The next day there came a young Woman a Kinswoman of the said *Amy*, and a neighbour of this Deponent, and told this Deponent, that her Aunt (meaning the said *Amy*) was in a most lamentable condition having her face all scorched with fire, and that she was sitting alone in her House, in her smock without any fire. And thereupon this Deponent went into the House of the said *Amy Duny* to see her, and found her in the same condition as was related to her;

for her Face, her Leggs, and Thighs, which this Deponent saw, seemed very much scorched and burnt with Fire, at which this Deponent seemed much to wonder. And asked the said *Amy* how she came into that sad condition? and the said *Amy* replied, she might thank her for it, for that she this Deponent was the cause thereof, but that she should live to see some of her Children dead, and she upon Crutches. And this Deponent farther saith, that after the burning of the said Toad, her Child recover'd, and was well again, and was living at the time of the Assizes. And this Deponent farther saith, That about the 6th. of *March*, 11º. *Car.* 2. her Daughter *Elizabeth Durent*, being about the Age of Ten Years, was taken in like manner as her first

first Child was, and in her fits complained much of *Amy Duny*, and said, That she did appear to her, and Afflict her in such manner as the former. And she this Deponent going to the Apothecaries for some thing for her said Child, when she did return to her own House, she found the said *Amy Duny* there, and asked her what she did do there? and her answer was, *That she came to see her Child, and to give it some water.* But she this Deponent was very angry with her, and thrust her forth of her doors, and when she was out of doors, she said, *You need not be so angry, for your Child will not live long*: and this was on a *Saturday*, and the Child dyed on the *Monday* following. The cause of whose Death this Deponent verily believeth

lieveth was occasion'd by the Witchcraft of the said *Amy Duny*: for that the said *Amy* hath been long reputed to be a *Witch*, and a person of very evil behaviour, whose Kindred and Relations have been many of them accused for *Witchcraft*, and some of them have been Condemned.

The said Deponent further saith, that not long after the death of her Daughter *Elizabeth Durent*, she this Deponent was taken with a Lameness in both her Leggs, from the knees downward, that she was fain to go upon Cruches, and that she had no other use of them but only to bear a little upon them till she did remove her Crutches, and so continued till the time of the Assizes, that the *Witch* came to be Tryed, and was there upon her

Churches,

Crutches; the Court asked her, *That at the time she was taken with this Lameness, if it were with her according to the Custom of Women?* Her Answer was, that it was so, and that she never had any stoppages of those things, but when she was with Child.

This is the Substance of her Evidence to this Indictment.

There was one thing very remarkable, that after she had gone upon Crutches for upwards of Three Years, and went upon them at the time of the Assizes in the Court when she gave her Evidence, and upon the Juries bringing in their Verdict, by which the said *Amy Duny* was found Guilty, to the great admiration of all Persons, the said *Dorothy Durent* was restored to the use of her Limbs, and went home with-

without making use of her Crutches.

II. As concerning *Elizabeth* and *Deborah Pacy*, the first of the Age of Eleven Years, the other of the age of Nine Years or thereabouts: as to the Elder, she was brought into the Court at the time of the Instructions given to draw up the Indictments, and afterwards at the time of Tryal of the said Prisoners, but could not speak one Word all the time, and for the most part she remained as one wholly senseless as one in a deep Sleep, and could move no part of her body, and all the Motion of Life that appeared in her was, that as she lay upon Cushions in the Court upon her back, her stomack and belly by the drawing of her breath, would arise

arise to a great height: and after the said *Elizabeth* had lain a long time on the Table in the Court, she came a little to her self and sate up, but could neither see nor speak, but was sensible of what was said to her, and after a while she laid her Head on the Bar of the Court with a Cushion under it, and her hand and her Apron upon that, and there she lay a good space of time: and by the direction of the Judg, *Amy Duny* was privately brought to *Elizabeth Pacy*, and she touched her hand; whereupon the Child without so much as seeing her, for her Eyes were closed all the while, suddenly leaped up, and catched *Amy Duny* by the hand, and afterwards by the face; and with her Nails scratched her till Blood came, and would by no means leave her till she was taken from her, and afterwards the Child would still be pressing towards her, and making signs of Anger conceived against her.

Deborah the younger Daughter was held in such extream manner, that her Parents wholly despaired of her life, and therefore could not bring her to the Assizes.

A Tryal of Witches. 15

The Evidence which was given concerning these Two Children was to this Effect.

Samuel *Pacy* a Merchant of *Leystoff* aforesaid, (a man who carried himself with much soberness during the Tryal, from whom proceeded no words either of Passion or Malice, though his Children were so greatly Afflicted,) Sworn and Examined, Deposeth, That his younger Daughter *Deborah*, upon *Thursday* the Tenth of *October* last, was suddenly taken with a Lameness in her Leggs, so that she could not stand, neither had she any strength in her Limbs to support her, and so she continued until the Seventeenth day of the same Month,

Month, which day being fair and Sunshiny, the Child desired to be carryed on the *East* part of the House, to be set upon the Bank which looketh upon the Sea; and whil'st she was sitting there, *Amy Duny* came to this Deponents House to buy some Herrings, but being denyed she went away discontented, and presently returned again, and was denyed, and likwise the third time and was denyed as at first; and at her last going away, she went away grumbling; but what she said was not perfectly understood. But at the very same instant of time, the said Child was taken with most violent fits, feeling most extream pain in her Stomach, like the pricking of Pins, and Shreeking out in a most dreadful manner like unto a Whelp,

Whelp, and not like unto a sensible Creature. And in this extremity the Child continued to the great grief of the Parents until the Thirtieth of the same Month. During this time this Deponent sent for one Dr. *Feavor*, a Doctor of Physick, to take his advice concerning his Childs Distemper; the Doctor being come, he saw the Child in those fits, but could not conjecture (as he then told this Deponent, and afterwards affirmed in open Court, at this Tryal) what might be the cause of the Childs Affliction. And this Deponent farther saith, That by reason of the circumstances aforesaid, and in regard *Amy Duny* is a Woman of an ill Fame, & commonly reported to be a *Witch & Sorceress*, and for that the said Child in her fits would cry out of *Amy Duny* as

C the

the cause of her Malady, and that she did affright her with Apparitions of her Person (as the Child in the intervals of her fits related) he this Deponent did suspect the said *Amy Duny* for a *Witch*, and charged her with the injury and wrong to his Child, and caused her to be set in the Stocks on the Twenty eighth of the same *October*: and during the time of her continuance there, one *Alice Letteridge* and *Jane Buxton* demanding of her (as they also affirmed in Court upon their Oathes) what should be the reason of Mr. *Pacy*'s Childs Distemper? telling her, That she was suspected to be the cause thereof; she replyed, *Mr. Pacy keeps a great stir about his Child, but let him stay until he hath done as much by his Children, as I have done by mine.* And being further

further examined, what she had done to her Children? She answered, *That she had been fain to open her Child's Mouth with a Tap to give it Victuals.*

And the said Deponent further deposeth, That within two days after speaking of the said words being the Thirtieth of *October*, the eldest Daughter *Elizabeth*, fell into extream fits, insomuch, that they could not open her Mouth to give her breath, to preserve her Life without the help of a Tap which they were enforced to use; and the younger Child was in the like manner Afflicted, so that they used the same also for her Relief.

And further the said Children being grievously afflicted would severally complain in their extremity, and also in the intervals, That

That *Amy Duny* (together with one other Woman whose person and Cloathes they described) did thus Afflict them, their Apparitions appearing before them, to their great terrour and affrightment: And sometimes they would cry out, saying, *There stands* Amy Duny, *and there* Rose Cullender; the other Person troubling them.

Their fits were various, sometimes they would be lame on one side of their Bodies, sometimes on the other: sometimes a soreness over their whole Bodies, so as they could endure none to touch them: at other times they would be restored to the perfect use of their Limbs, and deprived of their Hearing; at other times of their Sight, at other times of their Speech; sometimes by the

space

space of one day, sometimes for two; and once they were wholly deprived of their *Speech* for Eight days together, and then restored to their *Speech* again. At other times they would fall into *Swounings*, and upon the recovery to their *Speech* they would Cough extreamly, and bring up much *Flegme*, and with the same crooked *Pins*, and one time a *Two-penny Nail* with a very broad head, which *Pins* (amounting to Forty or more) together with the *Two-penny Nail* were produced in Court, with the affirmation of the said Deponent, that he was present when the said *Nail* was Vomited up, and also most of the *Pins*. Commonly at the end of every fit they would cast up a *Pin*, and sometimes they would have four or five fits in one day.

In this manner the said Children continued with this Deponent for the space of two Months, during which time in their Intervals this Deponent would cause them to Read some Chapters in the *New Testament*. Whereupon this Deponent several times observed, that they would read till they came to the Name of Lord, or Jesus, or Christ; and then before they could pronounce either of the said Words they would suddenly fall into their fits. But when they came to the Name of Satan, or Devil, they would clap their Fingers upon the Book, crying out, *This bites, but makes me speak right well.*

At such time as they be recovered out of their fits (occasion'd as this Deponent conceives upon their naming of Lord, or Jesus, or Christ,)

Christ,) this Deponent hath demanded of them, what is the cause they cannot pronounce those words, They reply and say, *That* Amy Duny *saith, I must not use that name.*

And farther, the said Children after their fits were past, would tell, how that *Amy Duny*, and *Rose Cullender* would appear before them, holding their Fists at them, threatning, *That if they related either what they saw or heard, that they would Torment them Ten times more than ever they did before.*

In their fits they would cry out, *There stands* Amy Duny, *or* Rose Cullender; and sometimes in one place and sometimes in another, running with great violence to the place where they fancied them to stand, striking at them as if if they were present; they would appear to them sometimes spinning, and sometimes reeling, or in other postures, deriding or threatning them.

And this Deponent farther saith, That his Children being thus Tormented by all the space aforesaid, and finding no hopes of amendment, he sent them to his Sisters House, one *Margaret Arnold*, who lived at *Yarmouth*, to make tryal, whether the change of the Air might do them any good. And how, and in what manner they were afterwards held, he this Deponent refers himself to the Testimony of his said Sister.

Margaret Arnold, Sworn and Examined, saith, That the said *Elizabeth* and *Deborah Pacy* came to her House about the Thirtieth

eth of *November* last, her Brother acquainted her, that he thought they were Bewitch'd, for that they vomited Pins; and farther Informed her of the several passages which occurred at his own House. This Deponent said, that she gave no credit to that which was related to her, conceiving possibly the Children might use some deceit in putting Pins in their mouths themselves. Wherefore this Deponent unpinned all their Cloathes, and left not so much as one Pin upon them, but sewed all the Clothes they wore, instead of pinning of them. But this Deponent saith, that notwithstanding all this care and circumspection of hers, the Children afterwards raised at several times at least Thirty Pins in her presence, and had most fierce and

and violent Fitts upon them.

The Children would in their Fitts cry out againſt *Roſe Cullender* and *Amy Duny*, affirming that they ſaw them; and they threatned to Torment them Ten times more, if they complained of them. At ſome times the Children (only) would ſee things run up and down the Houſe in the appearance of Mice; and one of them ſuddainly ſnapt one with the Tongs, and threw it into the fire, and it ſcreeched out like a Rat.

At another time, the younger Child being out of her Fitts went out of Doors to take a little freſh Air, and preſently a little thing like a Bee flew upon her Face, and would have gone into her Mouth, whereupon the Child ran in all haſte to the door to get into

A Tryal of Witches. 27

into the House again, screeking out in a most terrible manner; whereupon, this Deponent made haste to come to her, but before she could get to her, the Child fell into her swooning Fitt, and at last with much pain straining herself, she vomited up a Two-penny Nail with a broad Head; and after that the Child had raised up the Nail she came to her understanding; and being demanded by this Deponent, how she came by this Nail? she Answered, *That the Bee brought this Nail and forced it into her Mouth.*

And at other times, the Elder Child declared unto this Deponent, that during the time of her Fitts, she saw Flies come unto her, and bring with them in their Mouthes crooked Pins; and after the Child had thus declared the

the same, she fell again into violent Fits, and afterwards raised several Pins.

At another time, the said Elder Child declared unto this Deponent, and sitting by the Fire suddainly started up and said, *she saw a Mouse*, and she crept under the Table looking after it, and at length, she put something in her Apron, saying, *she had caught it*; and immediatly she ran to the Fire and threw it in, and there did appear upon it to this Deponent, like the flashing of Gunpowder, though she confessed she saw nothing in the Childs Hand.

At another time the said Child being speechless, but otherwise, of perfect understanding, ran round about the House holding her Apron, crying *hush, hush*, as if if there had been some Poultrey in the House; but this Deponent could perceive nothing: but at last she saw the Child stoop as if she had catch't at something, and put it into her Apron, and afterwards made as if she had thrown it into the Fire: but this Deponent could not discover any thing: but the Child afterwards being restored to her speech, she this Deponent demanded of her what she saw at the time she used such a posture? who answered, *That she saw a Duck.*

At another time, the Younger daughter being recovered out of her Fitts, declared, *That Amy Duny had been with her, and that she tempted her to Drown her self, and to cut her Throat, or otherwise to Destroy her self.*

At another time in their Fitts they

they both of them cryed out upon *Rose Cullender* and *Amy Duny*, complaining against them; *Why do not you come your selves, but send your Imps to Torment us?*

These several passages as most remarkable, the said Deponent did particularly set down as they daily happen'd, and for the reasons aforesaid, she doth verily believe in her conscience, that the Children were bewitched, and by the said *Amy Duny*, and *Rose Cullender*; though at first she could hardly be induced to believe it.

As concerning *Ann Durent*, one other of the Parties, supposed to be bewitched, present in Court.

Edmund Durent her Father Sworn and Examined; said, That he also lived in the said, Town of *Leystoff*, and that the said *Rose Cullender*, about the latter end

A Tryal of Witches.   31

end of *November* laſt, came into this Deponents Houſe to buy ſome Herrings of his Wife, but being denyed by her, the ſaid *Roſe* returned in a diſcontented manner; and upon the firſt of *December* after, his Daughter *Ann Durent* was very ſorely Afflicted in her Stomach, and felt great pain, like the pricking of Pins, and then fell into ſwooning fitts, and after the Recovery from her Fitts, ſhe declared, *That ſhe had ſeen the Apparition of the ſaid* Roſe, *who threatned to Torment her.* In this manner ſhe continued from the firſt of *December*, until this preſent time of Tryal; having likewiſe vomited up divers Pins (produced here in Court.) This Maid was preſent in Court, but could not ſpeak to declare her knowledge, but fell into moſt violent

violent fits when she was brought before *Rose Cullender.*

Ann Baldwin Sworn and Examined, Deposeth the same thing as touching the Bewitching of the said *Ann Durent.*

As concerning *Jane Bocking* who was so weak, she could not be brought to the Assizes.

Diana Bocking Sworn and Examined, Deposed, That she lived in the same Town of *Leystoff*, and that her said Daughter having been formerly Afflicted with swooning fitts recovered well of them, and so continued for a certain time; and upon the First of *February* last, she was taken also with great pain in her Stomach, like pricking with Pins; and afterwards fell into swooning fitts and so continued till the Deponents coming to the Assizes, having

ving during the same time taken little or no food, but daily vomiting crooked Pins; and upon Sunday last raised Seven Pins. And whilst her fits were upon her she would spread forth her Arms with her hands open, and use postures as if she catched at something, and would instantly close her hands again; which being immediatly forced open, they found several Pins diversly crooked, but could neither see nor perceive how or in what manner they were conveyed thither. At another time, the same *Jane* being in another of her fitts, talked as if she were discoursing with some persons in the Room, (though she would give no answer nor seem to take notice of any person then present) and would in like manner cast abroad her Arms,

Arms, saying, *I will not have it, I will not have it;* and at last she said, *Then I will have it,* and so waving her Arm with her hand open, she would presently close the same, which instantly forced open, they found in it a Lath-Nail. In her fitts she would frequently complain of *Rose Cullender* and *Amy Duny,* saying, That *now she saw* Rose Cullender *standing at the Beds feet, and another time at the Beds-head, and so in other places.* At last she was stricken Dumb and could not speak one Word, though her fitts were not upon her, and so she continued for some days, and at last her speech came to her again, and she desired her Mother to get her some Meat; and being demanded the reason why she could not speak in so long time? She answered

answered, *That Amy Duny would not suffer her to speak.* This Lath-Nail, and divers of the Pins were produced in Court.

As concerning *Susan Chandler,* one other of the Parties supposed to be Bewitched and present in Court.

Mary Chandler Mother of the said *Susan,* Sworn and Examined, Deposed and said, That about the beginning of *February* last past, the said *Rose Cullender* and *Amy Duny* were Charged by Mr. *Samuel Pacy* for Bewitching of his Daughters. And a Warrant being granted at the request of the said Mr. *Pacy,* by Sir *Edmund Bacon* Baronet, one of the Justices of the Peace for the County of *Suffolk* to bring them before him, and they being brought before him were Examined, and Confessed nothing

nothing. He gave order that they should be searched; whereupon this Deponent with five others were appointed to do the same: and coming to the House of *Rose Cullender*, they did acquaint her with what they were come about, and asked whether she was contented that they should search her? she did not oppose it, whereupon, they began at her Head, and so stript her naked, and in the lower part of her Belly they found a thing like a Teat of an Inch long, they questioned her about it, and she said, *That she had got a strain by carrying of water which caused that Excrescence.* But upon narrower search, they found in her Privy Parts three more Excrescencies or Teats, but smaller than the former: This Deponent farther saith, That in the

the long Teat at the end thereof there was a little hole, and it appeared unto them as if it had been lately sucked, and upon the straining of it there issued out white milkie Matter.

And this Deponent farther saith, That her said Daughter (being of the Age of Eighteen Years) was then in Service in the said Town of *Leystoff*, and rising up early the next Morning to Wash, this *Rose Cullender* appeared to her, and took her by the hand, whereat she was much affrighted, and went forthwith to her Mother, (being in the same town) and acquainted her with what she had seen; but being extreamly terrified, she fell extream sick, much grieved at her Stomach; and that Night after being in Bed with another young Woman,

Woman, she suddenly scrieked out, and fell into such extream fits as if she were distracted, crying against *Rose Cullender*; saying, *she would come to bed to her.* She continued in this manner beating and wearing her self, insomuch, that this Deponent was glad to get help to attend her. In her Intervals she would declare, *That some time she saw* Rose Cullender, *at another time with a great Dog with her*: She also vomited up divers crooked Pins; and sometimes she was stricken with blindness, and at another time she was Dumb, and so she appeared to be in Court when the Tryal of the Prisoners was; for she was not able to speak her knowledge; but being brought into the Court at the Tryal, she suddenly fell into her fits, and being

ing carryed out of the Court again, within the space of half an hour she came to her self and recovered her speech, and thereupon was immediatly brought into the Court, and asked by the Court, whether she was in condition to take an Oath, and to give Evidence, she said she could. But when she was Sworn, and asked what she could say against either of the Prisoners? before she could make any answer, she fell into her fits, screeking out in a miserable manner, crying *Burn her, burn her*, which were all the Words she could speak.

Robert Chandler father of the said *Susan* gave in the same Evidence, that his Wife *Mary Chandler* had given; only as to the searching of *Rose Cullender* as aforesaid.

This was the fum and Subſtance of the Evidence which was given againſt the Priſoners concerning the Bewitching of the Children before mentioned. At the hearing this Evidence there were divers known perſons, as Mr. Serjeant *Keeling*, Mr. Serjeant *Earl*, and Mr. Serjeant *Barnard*, preſent. Mr. Serjeant *Keeling* ſeemed much unſatisfied with it, and thought it not ſufficient to Convict the Priſoners: for admitting that the Children were in Truth Bewitched, yet ſaid he, it can never be applyed to the Priſoners, upon the Imagination only of the Parties Afflicted; For if that might be allowed, no perſon whatſoever can be in ſafety, for perhaps they might fancy another perſon, who might altogether be innocent in ſuch matters. There

There was also Dr. *Brown* of *Norwich*, a Person of great knowledge; who after this Evidence given, and upon view of the three persons in Court, was desired to give his Opinion, what he did conceive of them: and he was clearly of Opinion, that the persons were Bewitched; and said, That in *Denmark* there had been lately a great Discovery of Witches, who used the very same way of Afflicting Persons, by conveying Pins into them, and crooked as these Pins were, with Needles and Nails. And his Opinion was, That the Devil in such cases did work upon the Bodies of Men and Women, upon a Natural Foundation, (that is) to stir up, and excite such humours super-abounding in their Bodies to a great excess, whereby by he did in an extraordinary manner Afflict them with such Distempers as their Bodies were most subject to, as particularly appeared in these Children; for he conceived, that these swouning Fits were Natural, and nothing else but that they call the Mother, but only heightned to a great excess by the subtilty of the Devil, co-operating with the Malice of these which we term Witches, at whose Instance he doth these Villanies.

Besides the particulars abovemention'd touching the said persons Bewitched, there were many other things Objected against them for a further proof and manifestation that the said Children were Bewitched.

As *First*, during the time of the Tryal, there were some experiments

periments made with the Persons Afflicted, by bringing the Persons to touch them; and it was observed, that when they were in the midst of their Fitts, to all Mens apprehension wholly deprived of all sense and understanding, closing their Fists in such manner, as that the strongest Man in the Court could not force them open; yet by the least touch of one of these supposed Witches, *Rose Cullender* by Name, they would suddenly shriek out opening their hands, which accident would not happen by the touch of any other person.

And least they might privatly see when they were touched, by the said *Rose Cullender*, they were blinded with their own Aprons, and the touching took the same Effect as before.

There

There was an ingenious person that objected, there might be a great fallacy in this experiment, and there ought not to be any stress put upon this to Convict the Parties, for the Children might counterfeit this their Distemper, and perceiving what was done to them, they might in such manner suddenly alter the motion and gesture of their Bodies, on purpose to induce persons to believe that they were not natural, but wrought strangely by the touch of the Prisoners.

Wherefore to avoid this scruple it was privatly desired by the Judge, that the Lord *Cornwallis*, Sir *Edmund Bacon*, and Mr. Serjeant *Keeling*, and some other Gentlemen there in Court, would attend one of the Distempered persons in the farther part of the Hall,

Hall, whilst she was in her fits, and then to send for one of the Witches, to try what would then happen, which they did accordingly: and *Amy Duny* was conveyed from the Bar and brought to the Maid: they put an Apron before her Eyes, and then one other person touched her hand, which produced the same effect as the touch of the Witch did in the Court. Whereupon the Gentlemen returned, openly protesting, that they did believe the whole transaction of this business was a meer Imposture.

This put the Court and all persons into a stand. But at length Mr. *Pacy* did declare, That possibly the Maid might be deceived by a suspition that the Witch touched her when she did not. For he had observed divers times,

that

that although they could not speak, but were deprived of the use of their Tongues and Limbs, that their underſtandings were perfect, for that they have related divers things which have been when they were in their fits, after they were recovered out of them. This ſaying of Mr. *Pacy* was found to be true afterwards, when his Daughter was fully recovered (as ſhe afterwards was) as ſhall in due time be related: For ſhe was asked, whither ſhe did hear and underſtand any thing that was done and acted in the Court, during the time that ſhe lay as one deprived of her underſtanding? and ſhe ſaid, *ſhe did*: and by the Opinions of ſome, this experiment, (which others would have a Fallacy) was rather a confirmation that the Parties were really

really Bewitched, than otherwise: for say they, it is not possible that any should counterfeit such Distempers, being accompanied with such various Circumstances, much less Children; and for so long time, and yet undiscovered by their Parents and Relations: For no man can suppose that they should all Conspire together, (being out of several families, and, as they Affirm, no way related one to the other, and scarce of familiar acquaintance) to do an Act of this nature whereby no benefit or advantage could redound to any of the Parties, but a guilty Conscience for Perjuring themselves in taking the Lives of two poor simple Women away, and there appears no Malice in the Case. For the Prisoners themselves did scarce so much as Object

ject it. Wherefore, say they, it is very evident that the Parties were Bewitched, and that when they apprehend or understand by any means, that the persons who have done them this wrong are near, or touch them; then their spirits being more than ordinarily moved with rage and anger at them being present, they do use more violent gestures of their Bodies, and extend forth their hands, as desirous to lay hold upon them; which at other times not having the same occasion, the instance there falls not out the same.

2*ly.* One *John Soam* of *Leystoff* aforesaid, Yeoman, a sufficient Person, Deposeth, That not long since, in harvest time he had three Carts which brought home his Harvest, and as they were going into

into the Field to load, one of the Carts wrenched the Window of *Rose Cullenders* House, whereupon she came out in a great rage and threatned this Deponent for doing that wrong, and so they passed along into the Fields and loaded all the Three Carts, the other two Carts returned safe home, and back again, twice loaded that day afterwards; but as to this Cart which touched *Rose Cullenders* House, after it was loaded, it was overturned twice or thrice that day; and after that they had loaded it again the second or third time, as they brought it through the Gate which leadeth out of the Field into the Town, the Cart stuck so fast in the Gates-head, that they could not possibly get it through, but were inforced to cut down the

the Post of the Gate to make the Cart pass through, although they could not perceive that the Cart did of either side touch the Gate-posts. And this Deponent further saith, That after they had got it through the Gate-way, they did with much difficulty get it home into the Yard; but for all that they could do, they could not get the Cart near unto the place where they should unload the Corn, but were fain to unload it at a great distance from the place, and when they began to unload they found much difficulty therein, it being so hard a labour that they were tired that first came; and when others came to assist them, their Noses burst forth a bleeding: so they were fain to desist and leave it until the next Morning, and then they

they unloaded it without any difficulty at all.

Robert Sherringham also Deposeth against *Rose Cullender*, That about Two Years since, passing along the Street with his Cart and Horses, the Axletree of his Cart touched her House, and broke down some part of it, at which, she was very much displeased, threatning him, that his Horses should suffer for it; and so it happen'd, for all those Horses, being Four in Number, died within a short time after: since that time he hath had great Losses by the suddain dying of his other Cattle; so soon as his Sows pigged, the Pigs would leap and caper, and immediately fall down and dye. Also, not long after, he was taken with a Lameness in his Limbs that he could neither go nor stand for some days. After all this, he was very much vexed with great Number of Lice of an extraordinary bigness, and although he many times shifted himself, yet he was not any thing the better, but would swarm again with them; so that in the Conclusion he was forc'd to burn all his Clothes, being two suits of Apparel, and then was clean from them.

As concerning *Amy Duny*, one *Richard Spencer* Deposeth, That about the first of *September* last, he heard her say at his House, *That the Devil would not let her rest until she were Revenged on one* Cornelius Sandeswell's *Wife*.

Ann Sandeswel Wife unto the above-said *Cornelius*, Deposed, That about Seven or Eight Years since, she having bought a certain number

A Tryal of Witches.

number of Geese, meeting with *Amy Duny*, she told her, *If she did not fetch her Geese home they would all be Destroyed*: which in a few days after came to pass.

Afterwards the said *Amy* became Tenant to this Deponents Husband for a House, who told her, *That if she looked not well to such a Chimney in her House, that the same would fall*: Whereupon this Deponent replyed, That it was a new one; but not minding much her Words, at that time they parted. But in a short time the Chimney fell down according as the said *Amy* had said.

Also this Deponent farther saith, That her Brother being a Fisherman, and using to go into the *Northern Seas*, she desired him to send her a Firkin of Fish, which he did accordingly; and she having

ving notice that the said Firkin was brought into *Leyſtoff-Road*, she desired a Boatman to bring it ashore with the other Goods they were to bring; and she going down to meet the Boat-man to receive her Fish, desired the said *Amy* to go along with her to help her home with it; *Amy* Replyed, *She would go when ſhe had it.* And thereupon this Deponent went to the Shoar without her, and demanded of the Boatman the Firkin, they told her, That they could not keep it in the Boat from falling into the Sea, and they thought it was gone to the Divel, for they never saw the like before. And being demanded by this Deponent, whether any other Goods in the Boat were likewise lost as well as hers? They answered, *Not any.*

This

This was the substance of the whole Evidence given against the Prisoners at the Bar; who being demanded, what they had to say for themselves? They replyed, *Nothing material to any thing that was proved against them.* Whereupon, the Judge in giving his direction to the Jury, told them, That he would not repeat the Evidencce unto them, least by so doing he should wrong the Evidence on the one side or on the other. Only this acquainted them, That they had Two things to enquire after. *First,* Whether or no these Children were Bewitched? *Secondly,* Whether the Prisoners at the Bar were Guilty of it?

That there were such Creatures as *Witches* he made no doubt at all; For *First,* the Scriptures had affirmed so much. *Secondly*, The wisdom of all Nations had provided Laws against such Persons, which is an Argument of their confidence of such a Crime. And such hath been the judgment of this Kingdom, as appears by that Act of Parliament which hath provided Punishments proportionable to the quality of the Offence. And desired them, strictly to observe their Evidence; and desired the great God of Heaven to direct their Hearts in this weighty thing they had in hand: *For to Condemn the Innocent, and to let the Guilty go free, were both an Abomination to the Lord.*

With this short Direction the Jury departed from the Bar, and within the space of half an hour returned, and brought them in both *Guilty* upon the several Indictments,

dictments, which were Thirteen in Number, whereupon they stood Indicted.

This was upon *Thursday* in the Afternoon, *March* 13. 1662.

The next Morning, the Three Children with their Parents came to the Lord Chief Baron *Hales*'s Lodging, who all of them spake perfectly, and were as in good Health as ever they were; only *Susan Chandler*, by reason of her very much Affliction, did look very thin and wan. And their friends were asked, At what time they were restored thus to their Speech and Health? And Mr. *Pacy* did Affirm, That within less than half an hour after the *Witches* were Convicted, they were all of them Restored, and slept well
that

that Night, feeling no pain; only *Susan Chandler* felt a pain like pricking of Pins in her Stomach.

After, they were all of them brought down to the Court, but *Ann Durent* was so fearful to behold them, that she desired she might not see them. The other Two continued in the Court, and they Affirmed in the face of the Country, and before the *Witches* themselves, what before hath been Deposed by their Friends and Relations; the Prisoners not much contradicting them. In Conclusion, the Judge and all the Court were fully satisfied with the Verdict, and thereupon gave Judgment against the *Witches* that they should be Hanged.

They were much urged to confess, but would not.

That Morning we departed for *Cambridge*, but no Reprieve was granted: And they were Executed on *Monday*, the Seventeenth of *March* following, but they Confessed nothing.

www.ingramcontent.com/pod-product-compliance
Lightning Source LLC
Chambersburg PA
CBHW032150160426
43197CB00008B/848